Coachwork by
Eastern Coach Works

By
Malcolm R. White
The Sea and Land Heritage Research Series
2007

Published by Malcolm R. White
Coastal Publications
71 Beeching Drive
Lowestoft
NR32 4TB
First Published July 2007
Copyright © Malcolm R. White 2007 All rights reserved

Printed by Microkpress Printers Ltd.
27 Norwich Road
Halesworth
Suffolk
IP19 8BX
ISBN 9780954732356

OTHER TITLES IN THIS UNIQUE SERIES

COLOUR KEY :- ———— = MARITIME   ———— = TRANSPORT   ———— = LOCAL HISTORY

CAPTIONS

Front Cover (Top Right) - Twenty four bodies were built at the factory for mounting on Leyland Tiger TS7 chassis in 1936-37 for East Yorkshire Motor Services. The bodies were finished in a number of different layouts and seating capacities. One of the twenty four, 315 (CKH243) is seen here at Hull in the late 1930s *(Allan Wood Collection)*

Front Cover (Top Left) - Complete with NBC and Tyne & Wear logos Cummins powered Northern General 3740 (B740GCN), an Olympian comprising chassis ONCL10/1RV ON1832 and body 26008, is ready to leave the factory for service with Tyne & Wear PTE on 28th March 1985 . *(Copyright Norman Fairhead)*.

Front Cover (Bottom) - The award winning Ebdon's coach with the ECW office building in the background. Details of this coach can be found on page 115. *(Copyright Norman Fairhead)*

Title Page - A typical scene in the early 1950s with a newly arrived chassis being checked prior to entering the factory for bodywork to commence. At that time it was normal for these to be driven from Bristol to Lowestoft with the unprotected driver exposed to the elements. In later years the chassis were delivered from the builders by lorry. *(Copyright Phillip Burcham)*

Opposite - Maintained to a very high standard this Bristol LH, previously Hants & Dorset 3547 (GLJ479N), is still at work together with others in Malta in 2007. Completed at ECW with B43F bodywork in December 1974, it has body 21339 carried on chassis LH6L LH-981 and now carries the Maltese registration EBY524. This scene was recorded on 28th February 2001. *(Copyright Malcolm White/Paul Simpson)*

CONTENTS

GENERAL INFORMATION

Every effort has been made to ensure that information contained in this publication is accurate and for this reason numerous sources been consulted. These include personal accounts of events, official documentation, local diaries, media and enthusiasts resources and numerous accredited research works. However, when considering such a complex, varied and historical subject with some details gathered from hand written records that were provided by other parties, 100% accuracy cannot be guaranteed. Books in this series are part of the National Published Archive and as such are included in the library collections of the British Library, the National Library of Scotland, the National Library of Wales, the Universities of Oxford and Cambridge, Trinity College, Dublin and, when appropriate, The National Museum of Science & Industry.

This series is published by an enthusiast for the enthusiast and not, as in the great majority of similar works, for financial gain for the author and a commercial publishing house. Any profit that does arise from the sale of books in this series is donated to charity and good causes.

PHOTOGRAPHIC OWNERSHIP AND COPYRIGHT

ACKNOWLEDGEMENTS

Much appreciated has been the cooperation and support offered during the preparation of this book by a number of kind people interested in recording the transport heritage of the area, or who are interested in the tens of thousands of vehicles with bodywork built at Laundry Lane/Eastern Way. These include in particular Mr. Norman Fairhead who has allowed complete access to his vast collection of photographs, memorabilia and artefacts relating to Eastern Coach Works and Mr. David Bullard for his comprehensive notes on many different aspects of working at Eastern Way and Economy Road. The successful completion of *Coachwork by Eastern Coach Works*, the sixteenth in this unique series, would not have been possible without the valuable help provided by Mr. Stuart Jones BA. Stuart has provided important editorial support for all 15 titles in the series and has done so again with this latest book.

Assisting either directly or indirectly in this complex project have been the East Anglia Transport Museum, Ipswich Transport Museum, Mr. Carl Baker, Mr. Dennis Carver, Mr. Peter Hansford, Mr. Peter Killby, Mr. Geoffrey Moore, Mr. Robert Ranger, Mr. John Wells, Mrs. Cathryn White, Mr. David White, Mr. Allan Wood and also the staff of the Lowestoft Record Office. In addition to the information sources already mentioned, detailed information about Eastern Coach Works products has been obtained from various PSV Circle booklets, fleet list books, *The Hooter, Leyland Bulletin - National, Leyland Bulletin - Eastern Coach Works* and many on-line information resources. These include those that give regular reports of the present ownership and whereabouts of Eastern Coach Works bodied vehicles and also those that give a comprehensive history of them. I am extremely grateful to those who take time to provide such interesting information for all to see worldwide.

Introduction

Many books and magazine articles have been published that feature the Eastern Coach Works (ECW); some of these have been similar in content and concentrated in very fine detail on the complex array of body styles, models and types produced at the Lowestoft factory from the very earliest years until closure. Others have included aspects of industrial relations at the plant, passed opinions on good and bad aspects of ECW designs and commented upon, in detail, the business and political aspects of the closure of this great vehicle body builder. It is perhaps surprising that these publications contain few photographs of the factory premises, buildings, the people who worked there and only one includes a plan of the factory site showing an early layout before it was greatly expanded. A different approach has been attempted with this book in that it looks at the subject from a local perspective.

Although providing an overview of the history of vehicle body building at Laundry Lane/Eastern Way, this book concentrates on the years that are within living memory of those that worked at ECW or folk who had relations that worked there and are no longer alive. With many large scale housing developments attracting numbers of new folk to the local area, it is now becoming more common for some people to have no knowledge of ECW, its products or where it was located.

For a number of years many readers of books in this series have asked when a locally produced book about Eastern Coach Works would be available. This year (2007) is the twentieth anniversary of the closure of the factory and an appropriate time to publish this much requested book. *Coachwork by Eastern Coach Works* includes aspects of the ECW history not previously covered and the opportunity has been taken to include hundreds of previously unpublished photographs taken at the factory. A large number of images of ECW bodied vehicles at work across the UK and some in preservation have been included.

I have a special interest in this once major employer since my father worked there all his life, mainly in the Body Shop. Consequently the daily talk in our house was about the buses and coaches being built there at the time and also whether any repair jobs, repaint work or rebuilds had come in from the large number of PSV operators across the country that had dealings with the famous factory. Today a large number of vehicles with bodywork constructed at the factory survive and indeed some are still in front line daily service. Due to their age, those still in service will no doubt be scheduled for early replacement by vehicles made to the latest European Union standards. To their great credit the preservation movement has accumulated, usually with limited funds, manpower and resources, a good representation of buses and coaches with Lowestoft built bodywork with examples of the last type, the Olympian, now joining the ranks of these vehicles. The Coach Works, whose quality products could be found throughout the United Kingdom and in a number of countries overseas is no more and even now, many years after the closure, it has still not been replaced as a major local employer or as a national and international ambassador for the town of Lowestoft.

I have been very privileged to include in this book some of the hundreds of images recorded by Mr. Norman Fairhead during the four years before the closure of Eastern Coach Works. These give a very valuable and unique insight into the factory at work and provide a marvellous and irreplacable record of an important aspect of bygone industrial Lowestoft.

This book has been published as a tribute to the thousands of highly skilled and dedicated folk who worked at the factory from its earliest days until the run down and total closure by Leyland in January 1987 and is designed to be of interest to those who worked there, had relations that worked there, transport enthusiasts and local historians. It also commemorates the twentieth anniversary of the untimely and short sighted closure of this very important manufacturing plant and town asset of which no trace now remains.

Malcolm White
Lowestoft
June 2007

Some Abbreviations found in this Book

AEC	Associated Equipment Company
B45	Leyland Olympian
B	Bristol chassis
BCV	Bristol Commercial Vehicles formerly the manufacturing side of Bristol Tramways & Carriage Co. Ltd.
BEF	British Electrical Federation
BET	British Electric Traction
BTC	British Transport Commission
DAB	Dansk Automobil Byggeri
ECOC	Eastern Counties Omnibus Company
ECW	Eastern Coach Works
FL	Flat floor Long - rear entrance
FLF	Flat floor Long - Forward entrance
FS	Flat floor Short - rear entrance
FSF	Flat floor Short - Forward entrance
G	Bristol chassis type
GER	Great Eastern Railway
H	Bristol chassis type
J	Bristol chassis type
K	Bristol chassis - variants KS and KSW
L	Bristol chassis type
LL	Longer version of the Bristol L chassis
LWL	Longer, wider version of the Bristol L chassis
LD	Bristol Low height double Deck or LoDekka chassis, see Note
LH	Bristol Light Horizontal chassis
LHS	LH Short version
LNER	London & North Eastern Railway
LS	Bristol Light Saloon chassis
MW	Bristol Medium Weight saloon chassis
N	Prototype Bristol VR chassis
NBC	National Bus Company
NUVB	National Union of Vehicle Builders
OMO	One Man Operation
PSV	Public Service Vehicle
PTE	Passenger Transport Executive
RE	Bristol Rear Engine. Single deck chassis
RELH	RE Long High floor chassis
RELL	RE Long Low floor chassis
RESH	RE Short High floor chassis
RESL	RE Short Low floor chassis
SC	Bristol Small Capacity saloon chassis
SELNEC	South East Lancashire North East Cheshire
SMT	Scottish Motor Traction

SU	Bristol Small Underfloor saloon (under floor engine) chassis
SUL	SU Long chassis
SUS	SU Short chassis
TBAT	Tilling and British Automobile Traction
VAM	Vauxhall chassis (VA series medium length)
VR	Bristol Vertical Rear. Rear engined double deck chassis. Originally N type.
VRT	Bristol Vertical Rear with Transverse engine
VRTLH	VRT Long High floor chassis
VRTLL	VRT Long Low floor chassis
VRTSL	VRT Short Low floor chassis

Note - Development of the LD led to several other variants including : - **FL, FLF, FS** and **FSF**

VEHICLE BODYWORK CODES

These are usually expressed as Body Type, Seating Capacity followed by Door Position. For example, ECW bodied London Buses Leyland Olympian double deck bus L108 (C108CHM), completed in July 1986, had body 26426 configured as H42/26D.

Letter(s) before the seating capacity figure

B	Single deck bus
BB	Beverley Bar roof design
C	Single deck coach
CH	Double deck coach
CO	Double deck bus with removable top
DP	Dual purpose vehicle
F	Full front design
H	Highbridge layout double deck bus
L	Lowbridge layout double deck bus
LD	Lowbridge double deck bus with highbridge type seating layout (as Bristol LD or Lodekka)
O	Permanent open top double deck bus
OB	Open top single deck bus
U	Utility (wartime) type body

Seating capacity

The seating capacity for double deckers is shown with the upper deck capacity followed by the lower deck, e.g. H41/32F.

Letter following the seating capacity indicates door position (s)

C   Central entrance
D   Front entrance, centre exit with platform doors
F   Front entrance/exit with platform doors
R   Rear entrance/exit, open platform
RD   Rear entrance/exit, platform doors

CODES FOR BRISTOL CHASSIS

Basic information describing the vehicle engine can sometimes be found in photographic captions and elsewhere.
For example, a Bristol FLF6G denotes a 6 cylinder Gardner engine. Other makes of engine codes include A - Albion for the Bristol SU or AEC for K and L types, B - Bristol AVW or BVW engines, L - Leyland and P - Perkins engines. Early Bristol chassis identification codes included the letter O i.e. GO5G. This signified an oil engine as opposed to petrol. This practice was dropped in the late 1930s, by which time oil engines had became standard.

The Bristol VR variants

The method of stating chassis types for the Bristol VR may appear complex but is quite straight forward considering the many options an operator could ask for with these vehicles. The format is VRw/xxx/yyy, where w is the engine orientation - T (transverse) or L (longitudinal). The prototypes carried an X here, i.e. VRX, xxx reflects the chassis details, and yyy the engine, e.g. VRT/SL3/6LXB is a short, low, Series 3 with a transverse Gardner 6LXB engine.
This particular chassis with ECW bodywork was the most common variant of the VR. Where a number follows the engine type identifier, this is the chassis number. Another method of describing a VRT chassis followed the traditional Bristol method, but did not include the series identifier or chassis number.
     e.g. VRT/SL6G is a VRT/Short Low 6 cylinder Gardner.

The chassis details reflected the many types available :-

LH	Long - High Series 1
LH2	Long - High Series 2
LL	Long - Low Series 1
LL2	Long - Low Series 2
LL3	Long - Low Series 3
SL	Short - Low Series 1
SL2	Short - Low Series 2
SL3	Short - Low Series 3

Standard VRTLL bodies were typically 32ft. 9½ ins. in length and standard VRTSL bodies were 30ft. 9ins., however this could vary according to the type and manufacturer of the windscreen fitted. The height of a body varied from 13ft. 5ins. for the ultra low body, to 14ft. 6ins. for the full height body. The standard body was 13ft. 8ins.

The engine options offered for the VR included power units produced by AEC, Gardner and Leyland. These gave rated outputs ranging from 112bhp (Gardner 6LW) to 180bhp (Gardner 6LXB). The Gardner engines were by far the most popular, but if a chassis had been fitted with a Leyland engine it would be indicated thus:-

    VRT/SL3/501 where 501 indicates the type of Leyland engine.

In the mid 1980s, one Series 3 VRT originally fitted with a Leyland 501 engine, was successfully fitted with a replacement Cummins unit.

Finally, six actual examples of an ECW method adopted to identify VR chassis :-

Body	Chassis	Date	Operator/Fleet No.
17269	VRT/SL/6G/114	1969	Thames Valley 500
19847	VRL/LH2/6L/148	1972	Standerwick 72
20001	VRT/SL2/6G/406	1973	SELNEC 400
22472	VRT/SL3/6LXB/1050	1978	Bristol 5527
22473	VRT/SL3/501/763	1977	Crosville DVL341
24500	VRT/SL3/6LXC/2835	1981	West. National 1234

This proved quite a simple and effective method of identification for the thousands of VR chassis bodied at ECW and contains a considerable amount of information.

Key
1 Canteen
2 Fitters Shop
3 Bonding Shop
4 Finished Parts Store
5 Panel Shop
6 Body Shop (Jigs)
7 Body Shop (Assembly)
8 Fibreglass Shop
9 Trimmers Shop
10 Paint Shop
11 Varnish Shop
12 Electricians Shop
13 Spray Booth
14 Tool Room
15 Sawmill
16 Sports Field
17 Vehicle Park
18 Bowling Green
19 Tennis Courts
20 Drawing Office
21 Setters Out

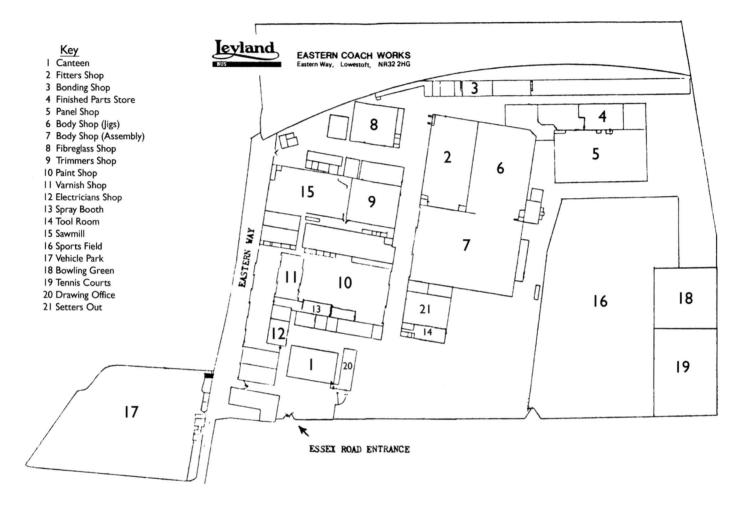

EASTERN COACH WORKS
Eastern Way, Lowestoft, NR32 2HG

EASTERN WAY

ESSEX ROAD ENTRANCE

1985
VISITORS GUIDE TO EASTERN COACH WORKS

EASTERN COACH WORKS
LIMITED
HEAD OFFICE & MAIN WORKS
EASTERN WAY
LOWESTOFT

The name of Eastern Coach Works was changed in 1975 when the word "Limited" was removed due to loss of the Limited Company status. (*ECW*)

A Brief History of Eastern Coach Works

Includes images of new vehicles on road test at various locations in the Lowestoft area.

This attractive scene was recorded in the last years of Eastern Coach Works.
(Copyright Norman Fairhead)

At one time the Eastern Coach Works (ECW) was the largest full time employer in Lowestoft with just over 1200 workers and a major contributor to the local economy. Unlike many other large local industries, the work was not seasonal and this leading UK vehicle body builder was usually kept very busy. ECW had a large supply chain that included some local firms, and at one time had a substantial output averaging in the region of 700 vehicle bodies per annum.

The factory in Eastern Way was finally closed by Leyland in January 1987 after several years of declining orders, job losses, general uncertainty over future prospects and a policy of the owners of moving work to other plants in the north. Many believe ECW became a victim of an accumulation of factors originating in boardrooms many miles from Lowestoft and that it should never have been closed. An increased demand for public service vehicle manufacturing capacity is now apparent, partly due to climate change and ever increasing traffic congestion and in this respect Eastern Coach Works is sorely missed.

With the passing of time and knowing how the bus manufacturing business has evolved, it is apparent that the factory was run down and closed so that other bus building plants could survive and prosper. The sale of Leyland Bus to Volvo so soon after they had closed and disposed of ECW, adds to the theory that some members of Leyland higher management had a long held agenda to dispose of the factory for a number of reasons, one of which was that it was not economically situated and could easily be replaced.

PART ONE - FROM THE BEGINNING TO 1940

ECW could trace its roots back to 4th April 1912, when a forerunner of the company, United Automobile Services Ltd., was formed with three directors, Mr. Ernest Boyd Hutchinson - Traffic Expert later Managing Director and General Manager, Mr. Andrew Miller Alexander - Chairman, and Mr. John Arnold - Engineer. The registered office of the Company was originally at 17 Gracechurch Street, London, E.C.1, but the administration was carried out from Lowestoft where the main office was located and where in May 1912, United Automobile Services (United) commenced operations in and around the town. The United fleet initially consisted of two second-hand Halley charabancs and two second-hand Commer charabancs. The vehicles were painted grey and were garaged in premises on Horn Hill in South Lowestoft; the services were advertised as being provided appropriately by Grey Cars. On 3rd September 1913 the registered office was transferred from London to Mill Road Garage, Lowestoft.

The Great Eastern Railway (GER) had been operating bus services in the Lowestoft area since July 1904 using three Milnes-Daimler double deck buses and this was the only competition that United faced. During January 1913, the GER discontinued their services in the Lowestoft area including that to Southwold. Their services, together with their garage and workshop in Denmark Road were taken over by the United. The small company office in Clapham Road, Lowestoft moved to the former railway premises in Denmark Road and the United fleet was garaged there in preference to the rented accommodation in south Lowestoft. As part of the move to Denmark Road the registered office was moved from Mill Road Garage to Great Eastern Garage, Denmark Road, Lowestoft on 19th September 1913.

Services operated by United in the early years included those to Southwold (service 1), Beccles (service 2), Oulton Broad (service 3) and Kessingland (service 4). The historic former GER/United garage building could be seen in Denmark Road until November 2005 when, after being badly damaged by fire, it was demolished. During October 1912, United commenced operations many miles from Lowestoft centred on Bishop Auckland in County Durham where a garage and small workshop were provided for the vehicles based there. Initially three local services were run in that area and these proved to be very successful, complementing the already successful East Anglian services based at Lowestoft. By the end of 1913, United had established depots at Bishop Auckland,

Durham, Lowestoft and Southwold. Unfortunately this success was not to continue when, with the outbreak of World War One, over half the fleet of around 27 operational vehicles were requisitioned for military use. With fuel in short supply, some of the remaining vehicles were converted to run on paraffin or coal gas thereby enabling limited services to be run.

Following the end of the war in November 1918, United pursued a policy of rapid expansion and in May 1919 purchased land in Laundry Lane, Lowestoft, to build garages, a stores building, a fitters shop and a machine shop. With the completion of this work, in December 1919, plans were released giving details of further buildings to be built on the site and these included a coach factory.

An indication of the tremendous rate of progress within United is that by 1919, the fleet totalled just over 60 vehicles, but within ten years this number would increase to around 600. The building of United bodies at Laundry Lane commenced in September 1920 with the first body being given the number 301 (Fleet No. B11). The chassis was a Daimler CB and the body was in B26F format. This was the start of a series of body numbers that ran until 1944, when a new series was introduced. Some of the early additions to the fleet were reconditioned War Department vehicles such as lorries and ambulances, which after conversion at their Lowestoft factory were suitable for use as "lorry buses", charabancs, buses and parcel vans. Others were purchased from the manufacturers' stocks of reconditioned War Department machines and

An "improved" Lorry Bus (Malcolm White Collection)

converted for passenger transport use at Lowestoft. In its most basic form, the "lorry bus" was a passenger carrying vehicle often fitted with wooden plank seats and a canvas tilt over a simple frame for weather protection. The company purchased large numbers of AEC Y-type and Daimler CB chassis and vehicles for conversion.

The facilities of the new coach factory enabled United to repair, refurbish and convert many war surplus vehicles thus enabling rapid growth in the United fleet and the replacement of some older vehicles. With expansion in mind and a large number of buses now available or under conversion, United established more services in East Anglia and in the north east in South Durham and Northumberland. To cater for the seemingly ever increasing fleet, the Company set up new workshops, repair facilities and a short lived body building factory at Bishop Auckland. Interestingly, some five years after the cessation of hostilities, many British Army motor vehicles were still to be found scattered across France and Belgium, some were in recognised dumps, and others apparently abandoned. Hutchinson arranged for over 140 AEC and a number of Daimler vehicles together with an assortment of other makes to be shipped back to the UK and then to Lowestoft for conversion on similar lines to the war surplus vehicles already dealt with a few years earlier. During this period of expansion at

Lowestoft, the registered office of United was transferred from there to 10/11 Billiter Square Buildings, London E.C.1.

The bodybuilding and repair facilities at Laundry Lane were kept separate, and by 1921, a small office had been added adjacent to the coach factory for use as the body building office. At this time the bodies built by the Company were single deck, constructed on timber frames using mass production methods and incorporating the use of jigs. Complete body sides and the roof were built flat and when each section had been completed it was assembled to form a whole body. This was then lifted into place onto an already prepared chassis.

In line with the policy of expansion, an associate company, W. T. Underwood, was formed to operate services in Derbyshire, Yorkshire and Lincolnshire in 1920 with headquarters at Clowne. World War One and the after effects did in no way change Hutchinson's enthusiasm to further expand United and by the late 1920s, it had developed into a very large concern operating bus services in many areas throughout eastern England from Southwold to the Scottish border in addition to having large modern "in house" vehicle body building facilities.

During January 1920, it was announced that a new large office block would be constructed on the Lowestoft site and this building later became the company registered office for a time,

Fleet No. A82 with possibly body 348 (Series 1), a former lorry bus fitted with a "Norfolk" body with removable upper deck, sides and seats.
(Malcolm White Collection)

Specific details of many early United vehicles are difficult to determine. Pre 1914 photographs show this body on a different chassis and A42 (AH0138) seems to have been rebuilt on a new AEC YB chassis in 1919 retaining the fleet and registration plates. *(Past Times Prints)*

prior to moving to Kilburn House in York during November 1926.

With the coach building factory now in full production, United were constructing a large number of bodies for fitting to chassis that included AEC, Daimler, Ford, Guy and White manufacture. At the 1921 Commercial Motor Show at London's Olympia, the box like bodies with arched tops to the windows were described as a 24-26 seat one man operated "Norfolk" Light Bus body. By 1924, a new body was available that appeared to have more style and appeal than the rather austere looking "Norfolk"; this was followed by a number of other designs catering for the rapidly changing public transport industry.

Records show that the seating capacity of the vehicles built between 1921 and 1925 ranged from 14 to 39 passengers and, whilst the great majority of bodies were equipped for use as buses, others were completed as charabancs or dual purpose chara-bus type vehicles. Initially vehicles had solid tyres but with advancing technology this policy was later changed to pneumatic tyres.

By the mid 1920s bodies were being produced for use on new chassis that were replacing the War Department variety and allowing a degree of standardisation to be introduced. With one exception, the early 1920s saw all of the production from the factory destined for their own fleet. The exception was a body built for the Derbyshire operator Underwood, a United

Fleet No. C72 (PW104), a Daimler CB chassis with body 402 (Series 1), an improved 1923 body design. (Malcolm White Collection)

subsidiary company. During 1923, United constructed an experimental 74 seat double deck centre staircase body for mounting on an AEC YC chassis. Named "Big Bertha" the bus was initially sent to Northumberland to work where it met local resistance and returned south to Lowestoft. It was employed on services to Southwold and Oulton Broad, but was later banned from Oulton Broad. Eventually "Big Bertha" was converted into a single deck bus and sent north again.

The Coach Factory commenced executing orders for other operators during 1924, the first being an order for sixteen bus bodies from Sunderland District Electric Tramways Ltd. Twelve of these were 26 seat bodies on AEC 202 chassis with pneumatic tyres, while the remaining four were 36 seat bodies on AEC 403 chassis with solid tyres. Also in 1924, the first order was received from United's first municipal customer when Great Yarmouth Corporation ordered seven bodies for mounting on Guy BB chassis.

Construction of vehicle bodies at Bishop Auckland did not last and after a short time the production of new bodies was concentrated at Lowestoft, with only maintenance and repair work being provided for in the north. Extra workers were taken on to cope with the increasing workload and during this period the workforce exceeded 300. United was consistently promoting vehicle body building in Lowestoft and advertising the factory as having the most modern plant, skilled workforce and the most up to date construction methods.

With a high degree of multiskilling, the workforce could be found maintaining, servicing and repairing the operational fleet and also building between 2 and 3 new bodies each week. Some of these workers were highly skilled shipwrights and ships carpenters who had left the local shipbuilding industry due to a lack of work. From this nucleus of employees it could be said that the Eastern Coach Works was formed and the manufacture of bus and coach bodywork firmly established in Laundry Lane.

The number of vehicles built using AEC chassis exceeded other makes and perhaps the reasons for this were that United was an agent for this chassis builder and a great many were available to buy cheaply. A number of motor car, lorry and van agencies were also held and these included AJS, Morris, Star, Hudson and Jowett. Sales and servicing for motor cars and commercials was at first carried out at premises adjacent to The Triangle in north

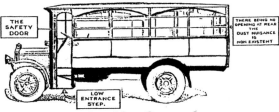

An advertisement for the United "Norfolk" bus body.
(Malcolm White Collection)

An advertisement for the Lorry Bus. Although this shows the Bishop Auckland address, similar advertisements displayed a Lowestoft address. Since some of the chassis are advertised as 1920 manufacture, these First World War bodies have apparently been placed on new chassis. One of the uses of these vehicles in wartime was as ambulances.
(Malcolm White Collection)

Lowestoft, but this later moved to Gordon Road in the former Regent Alfresco cinema, the site of this building now being included in Lowestoft Bus Station. Some of the rapid United expansion was due to the very successful policy of acquiring competitor's businesses, both in the north east and East Anglia. After the early years of successful development in East Anglia and with little competition left, the greatest area of opportunity for United was in the north. The United presence was widespread and by 1930, they had established 28 depots and many outstations in England including Attleborough, Blyth, Bridlington, Boston, Cromer, Darlington, Durham, Harleston, Hartlepool, Kings Lynn, London, Middlesbrough, Newcastle, Norwich, Ripon, Thirsk, Scarborough, Skegness, Southwold, Sunderland, Richmond, Wainfleet, Whitby and Whitley Bay. Providing public transport in such a vast area of England required a very large fleet, and the factory at Lowestoft played a substantial role in the remarkable United Automobile Services success story by having the capability to quickly build and repair company vehicles.

The Regent Garage, workshops and bus station in Gordon Road, Lowestoft, seen here when used by ECOC. At one time the Regent Alfresco theatre, the building was used during the late 1920s as a garage, workshop and sales area by United. *(Copyright Norman Fairhead)*

By 1925 it is known that at least 300 bodies had been constructed, most of these being for use in their own fleet. Bodywork repairs were being carried out on company and other operator's vehicles and the amount of work justified a further extension to the coach factory whose output at that time was four vehicles per week. Refurbishment of previously used chassis effectively ended in 1925 and in 1926 work started on a batch of one hundred half canopy 35 seat front entrance single deck bodies for fitting to new AEC 415 type chassis. This design was known as the "E" class and while most were finished as buses, others were charabancs which had fixed windows, removable canvas tops and a rear entrance. This was the first time that building large numbers of vehicles to a standard design had been attempted and the bodies were constructed using the usual wood and metal practice, with one body being constructed with a steel frame. All were placed in United service during 1926, a year when another move for the registered office took place. This time it moved from London to Kilburn House in Fulford Road, York. A batch of 140 bodies with standard seating for 39 passengers were built in 1927, for fitting to the ADC 415A chassis, a product of a joint venture between AEC and Daimler. The bodywork looked somewhat similar to the bodies produced the previous year.

A marked difference was seen in 1928 when a single deck 35 seat dual door full canopy body with a sloping windscreen was put in production. The body was mounted on another ADC chassis, the 425 and the resulting vehicle was most impressive and futuristic.

The late 1920s and early 1930s saw many bus, coach, charabancs and lorry bodies built at Laundry Lane for a wide range of customers using chassis produced by a range of manufacturers including ADC, AEC, Bristol, Chevrolet, GMC, Leyland, Maudsley, Star, Thornycroft and Tilling Stevens. Included in these were 10 bodies for the then independent Crosville Motor Services, an operator that would go on to have a very long association with the Lowestoft factory. Additions in 1928-29 to the United fleet included 125 dual entrance 35 seat bodies for mounting on ADC 425 type chassis, 20 coach bodies complete with toilets and pantries for use on long distance work and fitted to ADC 423 type chassis, and five 35 seat buses also with ADC 423 chassis. For use at Scarborough on the United sea front services, a number of specialised bodies were built for mounting on Daimler chassis.

The Laundry Lane factory was now well and truly established as one of the largest and most respected bus building plants in the country. At the same time, the United bus operating business was extensive and seen by some other public transport concerns as a possible threat. As a result in 1929, United Automobile Services became the subject of takeover bids from the London & North Eastern Railway (LNER) and also the Tilling and British Automobile Traction companies group (TBAT).

An example of the 1926 standard E class with ADC 415 chassis and United bodywork. *(Malcolm White Collection)*

The 20 seat Star VB, one of three built in 1928 with bodywork by United. *(Past Time Prints)*

The outcome of these two bids was that on 1st August 1929 United became jointly owned by TBAT and the LNER. TBAT was an organisation set up by Thomas Tilling Ltd. and British Electric Traction Co. Ltd. (BET) to control many of the major bus operators in England and Wales, while others were directly controlled by Tilling and by BET. Associated with BET was BEF (British Electrical Federation Ltd.), set up in 1907 as a purchasing and standards organisation within the BET Group. Body designs complying with BEF requirements had been built at the factory for many operators including Thames Valley, Western Welsh and Yorkshire Traction. Mr. E. B. Hutchinson resigned from the company and thus his fine leadership was lost. However, expansion continued in both operating and body building and by 1931 over 600 people were employed on body building by United at Laundry Lane. On the operational side in 1930 the company had acquired 390 vehicles, of which 120 were new. A positive outcome of the change of control was that the factory gained many new large customers within the Tilling group of companies and before long orders started to arrive. However, a reorganisation of the TBAT companies was approaching and the factory was directly involved. It was decided that the United Automobile Services operational area would in future be in the north and other TBAT companies would be responsible for the remaining areas.

Lincolnshire Road Car took over services in Lincolnshire on 1st January 1931 and the newly formed Eastern Counties Omnibus Company took over services in Norfolk and North Suffolk and some in the areas previously served by Ipswich, Cambridge and Peterborough based operators from 14th July 1931. Interestingly, Lincolnshire Road Car had been set up under the TBAT umbrella to take over an existing business in 1928 and in 1930 took over the business of Boston based Smiths. The transfer in 1931 saw 38 United vehicles of many different makes of chassis and bodywork pass to this operator. The Lowestoft factory passed into Eastern Counties Omnibus Company (ECOC) ownership in July 1931 and before long the name of the new owner was seen on the building in Laundry Lane together with the words "Coach Factory".

Similar in design to that displayed externally on United bodied vehicles, those built after the change of factory ownership to ECOC displayed this amended information notice. *(Malcolm White Collection)*

United AT80 was one of an order for 50 similar saloons ordered for its own fleet with delivery in 1930. The chassis used for these vehicles was the Leyland Tiger TS3. *(Malcolm White Collection)*

An unusual vehicle classed as a touring saloon was completed in 1932. Rather military in style, it was based on a Leyland Terrier 6 x 4 chassis and was for His Highness Abbas Helmi to use on safari. *(Past Times Prints)*

One of the first ventures into building double deck bodywork at Laundry Lane was when two orders for small numbers of buses using AEC Regent chassis were received, ironically both from local municipal operators within ten miles of the factory, Lowestoft Corporation Transport and Great Yarmouth Corporation Transport. An earlier trial in building a double deck body was not particularly successful.

Sales were to be restricted to associated companies within the TBAT group but orders received before the change in ownership were completed. In addition to Lowestoft taking delivery of eight AEC Regent 1 double deckers they also had four Guy FC single deckers in 1931, the bodywork of all these buses being recorded as having been constructed by United. An interesting point regarding the Lowestoft order was that of the eight double deckers, one had a diesel engine while the others were petrol driven. This bus was noteworthy in that it was reportedly the first diesel powered vehicle to have a body constructed at the factory. The buses had been purchased to replace the town's trams. The order from Great Yarmouth was for five AEC Regents and some vehicles from both orders were delivered after Eastern Counties had taken over control of the coach factory.

The years 1932-36 were an interesting period of expansion and development with orders from the following customers being received:-

Buses and Coaches

Birmingham & Midland	North Western
Brighton, Hove & District	Norwich Electric
Caledonian	Ribble
Crosville	Royal Blue
East Kent	Southern National
East Yorkshire	Southern Vectis
Eastern Counties	West Yorkshire
Eastern National	Western National
Hants & Dorset	TSM
Hebble	United
Keighley - West Yorkshire	United Services
Lancaster Mental Institution	Yorkshire Traction
Lincolnshire	Yorkshire Woollen
Maidstone & District	Westcliff on Sea
Morris	

Miscellaneous

Carrimore (Trailer)	Surtees (Lorry)
Cornish & Gaymer (Lorry)	Surtees (Van)
Haywood (Lorry)	United (Vans)
Hewett (Lorry)	Vince (Lorry)
H. H. Abbas Helmi (Special)	Woodgreaves (Lorry)
Ives (Van)	

The many different types of chassis used for the buses and coaches were manufactured by ADC, AEC, Albion, Bristol, Daimler, Dennis, Leyland, Morris, SOS, Thornycroft, Tilling Stevens and TSM.

Chassis used for the miscellaneous vehicles were manufactured by AEC (Mammoth, Matador, Mercury), Carrimore, Ford, Bedford, Chevrolet and GMC.

The Dennis Ace and the Mace were popular choices for some operators. This Ace, with body 3170 (Series 1) in B20F format, was one of many supplied to operators such as Western National, North Western, West Yorkshire, East Kent, Brighton Hove & District, Keighley -West Yorkshire and ECOC. *(Past Times Prints)*

Following the reorganisation of 1931, United moved their registered office from York to Grange Road, Darlington on 6th January 1932. Although no longer run by United, production at the Coach Factory did continue to include some of their designs. However, new ECOC designs appeared from 1932 and for a few years a mixture of old and new models could be seen at the Coach Factory. During the following five years the company experienced periods both of full employment and the occasional shortage of work, but the lean years of the early 1930's were successfully weathered with a diverse range of operators placing orders.

A "standard" design for double deck buses was actively promoted as a way of reducing costs and attracted substantial customer orders with many of these bodies being mounted on Leyland chassis. As the 1930s progressed, a feature of many of the chassis seen at the factory was that they were produced by the Bristol Tramways & Carriage Co. Ltd., another Tilling group company. Although slow to get established due to operators initially preferring other makes of chassis and some production difficulties, the Bristol/ECOC/ECW combination ran for many years and it can be said that of the tens of thousands of vehicles completed at the Lowestoft factory, the majority left the town displaying the familiar Bristol badge as well as the Coach Works badge. United were the first operator to use ECOC bodied Bristol

chassis when they ordered 20 saloons in 1933, the chassis used being the Bristol H type. This was accompanied by an order for bodywork of highbridge layout for mounting on eight petrol driven Leyland Titan TD2 chassis, the last United double deckers built before the changeover to diesel fuel.

In addition to supplying bodies for new chassis, ECOC were busy undertaking rebodying for a number of operators including some of their own. An assortment of former United vehicles had passed to ECOC when the reorganisation took place and many needed rebodying, amongst them United J class, K class and Daimler buses.

During the 1920s and 30s many tramway systems within the UK closed, leading to a demand for replacement buses from numerous operators. Typical of these was Yorkshire Electric Tramways (Woollen District) who ordered six Leyland Titan TD3 with ECOC double deck bodies for delivery in autumn 1934 and in York where the York - West Yorkshire Joint Committee placed orders with ECOC for bodies for tram replacement buses. A notable and some may say cute design emerged in 1934 that would become known as the "flying pig". This was intended for the small bus market with a 20 seat body on a Dennis Ace chassis. Within a short time the Ace was in great demand by many different operators. A half cab version of the Ace, the Mace, followed shortly afterwards.

Double deck bodies were supplied to Great Yarmouth Corporation on five AEC Regent chassis in 1931 during the time of the changeover from United to ECOC. These were not the first bus bodies to be built for this municipal operator at the factory, saloon bodies were supplied in 1924, 1927 and 1928. *(Malcolm White Collection)*

Western National 139 (OD7824) comprised Bristol H chassis H194 and body 3176(Series 1) configured as B32R. It was one of 24 supplied to that operator during August and September 1934. *(Malcolm White Collection)*

The year 1935 saw the first Bristol chassis fitted with a Gardner oil engine and to have bodywork constructed at Lowestoft when United were supplied with ten 48 seat double deck bodies on G type chassis. This arrangement of a Bristol chassis with a Gardner engine and ECOC or ECW bodywork would prove to be extremely popular, right up to the early 1980s. A number of existing ECOC designs were updated in the mid 1930s and others were changed as a result of operating experience. Included in these changes was the design for the "standard" double deck bus of which many by now were being built using Bristol chassis.

By 1935, the Coach Factory had become a very large concern and was supplying many public transport operators in the UK with quality vehicles built for a long life. With a workforce of almost 1,000, and an average output of 10 bodies per week, it was considered appropriate to change the structure of the company and create a separate vehicle body building subsidiary. On 1st July 1936, the coach and bus body building activities were segregated from the operating side of the business, formed into a limited company wholly owned by ECOC and registered as Eastern Coach Works Ltd. The new General Manager was Mr. William Bramham; previously General Manager of the well known

Leeds based vehicle builders Charles H. Roe Ltd. To increase sales opportunities it was decided to end the restrictions on the customer base and bodies would in future be produced for a much wider market including municipal undertakings. This policy of more aggressive marketing saw further expansion including a significant rise in the sale of bodies to operators belonging to the BET Group and an increase in the volume of work for Tilling associates. The main access road to the factory, until then known as Laundry Lane, was renamed Eastern Way at this time, but otherwise the day to day running of the factory changed little with the change of ownership and name. The general practice of building standard bodies for double deck buses and at the same time continuing to provide variable single deck body designs to meet operators own requirements, which started in the early ECOC days, continued to be well received by operators leading to the gaining of many orders from a wide range of customers. Amongst those received during 1935-36 was that from North Western with an order for single deck bodywork on seventy four Bristol JO5G chassis, Ribble with an order for twenty five front entrance 30 seat single deck bodies and eight 59 seat lowbridge double deck buses, and Crosville requiring 15 single deck bodies. Southern Vectis came forward with an order for six 56 seat highbridge double deck bodies on Dennis Lance 11 chassis for delivery in mid 1936. This useful order was followed by another from the same operator for two single deck buses, again using Dennis chassis.

York - West Yorkshire Y318 (AWW23) was one of 15 similar buses ordered for delivery in October 1935 for use in York. The chassis used was Bristol GO5G37 and the body 3943 (Series I), built to H32/28R format. A further order for ten other buses configured as L27/27R was completed in November 1935. *(ECW)*

Ribble 1622(RN7877) comprised Leyland LZ2 chassis 9380 and body 4249 (Series I) configured as B30F. It was one of 25 saloons supplied to Ribble by ECOC/ECW between May and November 1936. *(ECW)*

Many orders were in progress when the factory was renamed. The first double deck bodies built totally under ECW control were for eight highbridge buses with Bristol GO5G chassis and supplied to ECOC, and one similar vehicle supplied to Bristol as a demonstrator. The body was a splendid and impressive design and a good example of the work of the Lowestoft body builder. An interesting order from a municipal operator, Middlesbrough Corporation, was received in 1937 for six highbridge double deck bodies using Leyland Titan TD5 chassis. Previously a Roe customer, it was thought that Middlesbrough Corporation had placed the order as a result of previous dealings they had with Mr. Bramham at Roe, and by then the General Manager of ECW. This order was followed by further orders for the same operator for similar vehicles. Other municipals taking delivery of vehicles with ECW body work during this time included Burnley and Rochdale. Many orders were obtained during 1936-37, including those for coaches from Eastern National and Eastern Counties with Bristol chassis, it seemed that this chassis manufacturer was moving into a stronger position than it had previously had with the big fleet operators specifying that make. However, the 24 single deck vehicles, some finished as coaches and others buses, ordered by BET controlled East Yorkshire Motor Services during this period used Leyland Tiger TS7 chassis. The year 1937 saw the introduction of a series of new designs, some of which would continue to be built right up to the outbreak of the Second World War. An unusual order for three permanent highbridge open top bodies was received from Westcliff on Sea Motor Services for mounting on Bristol GO5G chassis. These vehicles went on to have very long lives, possibly due to their restricted seasonal use and mileage. Later, these classic vehicles became part of the Eastern National fleet. This Westcliff order followed an order in 1936 for three small single deck buses with Leyland Cub chassis. Also delivered to Westcliff in 1937 were ten 35 seat single deck bodies with Bristol JO5G chassis, an unusual feature of six of these was the folding canvas opening roof. Hebble ordered three single deck buses unusually with Albion chassis.

The years leading up to the Second World War saw the factory undertaking the fitting of many new bodies to older vehicles for a number of operators and continuing to supply large numbers of new quality bodies for both single and double deck vehicles

ordered by operators such as Black & White, Southern Vectis, Western Welsh, York-West Yorkshire, Brighton Hove and District, ECOC, Eastern National and Bristol. Of these perhaps the most luxurious were the eight 31 seat coach bodies with Bristol JO5G chassis supplied to Black & White in 1938, followed by a further six bodies for mounting on the new Bristol L6G chassis. These were well received partly due to the very large amount of leg room provided between the seats. The ECW design team was continuously updating, amending and producing new designs leading to success in attracting new orders for the factory and providing job security for the hundreds of employees. Largely unaltered for many years, the standard double deck bus design was modified around the upper deck windows, however the benefit of this change was short lived since that body was being phased out.

With the availability of the Bristol K type chassis, ECW unveiled a new very attractive and long lasting double deck design. Some features from the earlier standard double deck design were incorporated and these gave the new design a very distinctive appearance. West Yorkshire was one of the first operators to sample the delights of the new K type chassis and the newly designed standard bodywork when they ordered 21 of the new buses in 1937.

Middlesbrough Corporation was supplied with six 56 seat highbridge bodies on Leyland chassis in the summer of 1937. Repeat orders followed in 1938, 1939 and 1940. Seen here is Middlesbrough 73 (XG5233). *(ECW)*

The new Bristol single deck chassis, the L type, appeared in 1937. Two of the first large orders for ECW bodywork on the new chassis were for 36 vehicles for ECOC on the L4G chassis, and fifty 31 seat vehicles for North Western with L5G chassis in 1938. Both operators went on to order many more single deck vehicles with Bristol L type chassis and ECW body work. Changes in management occurred in 1938 when a new Works Manager was appointed to replace Mr. Cladish who left ECW for Windovers Ltd. a London based coachbuilder. The new Works Manager was a person familiar with the factory, Mr. Joseph Shirley(known to most as "Bill"). He had worked at ECW before moving to Leyland Motors as superintendent of the body shop in 1935. The last years of the 1930s saw the factory busy with a wide variety of orders and the outbreak of war on 3rd September 1939 initially made little difference to the output or quality of the products. With the country at war, many wondered if ECW would be able to continue to function and with this mind, provisional plans were drawn up to cater for a possible closure of the factory. In spite of many difficulties and awkward situations over which ECW had no control, a reduced but impressive output was achieved during 1938-42 with orders for bodywork completed for the following operators:-

Brighton, Hove & District	Rochdale
Bristol Tramways	Southern National
Caledonian	Southern Vectis
Crosville	Thames Valley
East Midland	Tyneside
East Yorkshire	United
Eastern Counties	United Counties
Eastern National	West Yorkshire
Hants and Dorset	Western National
Hebble	Western Welsh
Keighley - West Yorkshire	Westcliff on Sea
Maidstone & District	York - West Yorkshire
Middlesbrough	Yorkshire Traction
North Western	Yorkshire Woollen

Bodywork on single deck vehicles completed during this period at the factory included forty-nine 35 seat saloons for United Counties, twenty-eight 31 seat saloons for Eastern National and ten 35 seat saloons for East Midland. One aspect of wartime

conditions was that vehicles being built and leaving the factory had to have much reduced regulation lighting and restrictions were placed on the vehicle headlamps. During early 1939, Westcliff took delivery of three Bristol K5G double deck buses with folding roof tops and East Yorkshire took delivery of another unusual double deck design, the "Beverley Bar", the top of these vehicles being specially shaped to enable the bus to pass through a narrow and low gateway in the north of the town.

One interesting breakthrough in the few parts of the country not covered by Lowestoft bodied vehicles was when ECW supplied bodywork for 34 saloons with Leyland Tiger TS8 chassis that Maidstone & District ordered in 1938. With these buses in service, ECW bodywork was seen on a daily basis in Kent.

The first month of hostilities saw the first of eighteen 48 seat Bristol K5G double deck buses leave the factory for Thames Valley. In May 1940 the course of the war brought a dramatic change in the firm's expansion and steady growth in market penetration. Following the evacuation of the allied forces from Dunkirk and the feared invasion of this country, on the 27th of that month ECW received instructions from the military authorities to stop production immediately and clear the factory, with all wheeled vehicles being removed as far from Lowestoft as possible in order to deny their use to the enemy in the event of invasion. It is true to say that this instruction was not unexpected by many people since Lowestoft was the most easterly town in the UK and the local area was considered at high risk due to the possibility of enemy forces crossing the North Sea from occupied Europe. Due to men leaving the factory for military service and other tasks and air attacks on the town by enemy aircraft, production at ECW was at best described as difficult in the camouflaged buildings. During 1940, over 100 bombs were dropped on Lowestoft with air raids, and the subsequent stoppage of work, becoming a fact of life as the employees frequently disappeared into the factory air raid shelters. Only a small amount of damaged was caused to ECW by the many German bombs that were dropped in the vicinity of the factory. With the cooperation of the company's employees, the instructions to vacate the premises were completed in less than 24 hours. Following enquiries to find a new temporary home for ECW, a building at Irthlingborough in Northamptonshire was offered by United Counties as a possible answer. Previously used as a bus garage the building could be made available to ECW if they considered it appropriate. It had been built just before the First World War and extended in 1919 to double the original size. Built for Wellingborough Motor Services, the building passed to United Counties in 1921 and in addition to being used as a garage, it had been at one time used for body building and general repair workshops. As expected, the building would take some time to be made ready to accommodate the greatly downsized ECW. The clearout of ECW had to be completed before the new temporary premises were ready and homes had to found urgently for around 150 partially built vehicles that had to be removed from the factory. Those removed from the factory ranged from bare chassis to others approaching completion as buses or coaches. Operators, including United Counties, Eastern Counties, Eastern National, Brighton Hove and District and Bristol became involved, with some offering accommodation for vehicles still under construction and others offering to complete vehicles under supervision if possible. A major problem of temporary accommodation had been solved. A large amount of plant, stores, tools and machinery had to be removed from the Eastern Way premises with much of it destined for Irthlingborough. Some timber was sent initially to United Automobile Services premises in the north east prior to being sent on from there to Irthlingborough. With very little work available at the factory, the great majority of the ECW weekly paid employees together with many of its weekly paid staff were discharged, in total around 950 people being laid off.

The following month approximately 120 employees, including key men, supervisory and technical staff, were taken on to work at the smaller premises at Irthlingborough where a limited assembly line was to be set up. A small presence was maintained at the Lowestoft premises for security, fire watching and to undertake a small amount of vehicle body building and war effort related work. The temporary facilities at Irthlingborough were ready within six weeks for limited vehicle building work to commence; some of the first body work to be constructed was on fifteen partially completed highbridge double deck bodies for Rochdale Corporation. Vehicles completed by ECW during these difficult times were liable to be diverted to an operator that had the greatest need, regardless of who had placed the original order. In addition to a limited amount of new work and the arrival of unfinished bodies for completion from storage, repair and reconditioning work was carried out at Irthlingborough. A number of interesting tasks were carried out there including designing kits that would enable single deck buses to be converted into ambulances. The building at Irthlingborough was purchased by ECW in late 1941. Other novel projects entrusted to ECW during the war years included the experimental use of gas as a fuel for buses, and to determine the most efficient wartime use of a bus with regard to increasing the passenger carrying capacity. This last task involved altering the conventional seating pattern and included having seats positioned parallel to the vehicle sides in a perimeter style.

During 1938, ECW supplied bodywork for mounting on Bristol JO5G chassis for eight Black & White coaches. Black & White 86 (CDD1) was one of the batch of eight which was later followed by a further six on a different chassis. (ECW)

The interior of Black & White 86. (ECW)

Western National 217(ADV123) was one of twenty similar buses supplied to that operator in January and February 1936, with B32R bodywork on Bristol JO5G chassis. The body on 217 was 4119 (Series 1) and the chassis JO5G85. (ECW)

By 1935 the express services provided by Royal Blue were part of the Southern National and Western National operation. Eight coaches were ordered by Southern and Western National for use on Royal Blue services for delivery in March 1935. Four of the eight were destined for each of the operators, although the coaches had near identical livery. Royal Blue 165 (BTA455) was a Western National vehicle and comprised body 3487 (Series 1) and Bristol JJW176 chassis. At the rear of the roof the luggage carrier can be seen. This was accessed via a ladder mounted on the rear of the coach. (ECW)

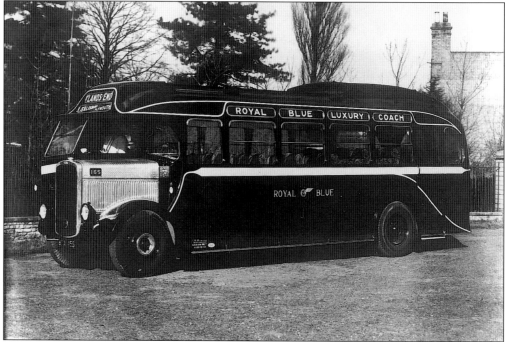

Yorkshire Traction 661 (HE9515) was one of six buses with H28/26R bodies delivered in late 1939 on Leyland TD5 chassis. No. 661 was fitted with body 6717 (Series 1). (ECW)

Hants & Dorset TD718 (ERU594) was one of 31 buses with L27/26R bodies ordered in 1939. The chassis used on 718 was Bristol K5G 49035 and the body was 6173 (Series 1). (ECW)

Tyneside 22 (JR8622) was one of eight highbridge buses supplied to Tyneside Tramways in 1938. The 56 seat bodies were fitted to Leyland Titan TD5 chassis. (ECW)

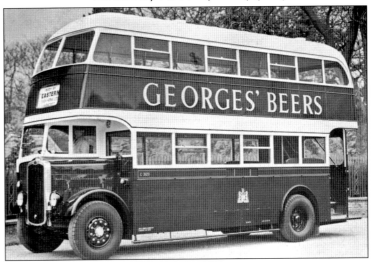

Bristol Tramways & Carriage Co. Ltd. C3120 (EHY582) was one of 54 supplied to that operator during 1938, The 56 seat body was fitted to a Bristol K5G chassis. (ECW)

The Dennis Mace was a larger half cab version of the Dennis Ace and handy for those operators where a 26 seat B26F bus was sufficient. Western National 601 (BTA61) was completed in November 1934 and one of 21 ordered by that operator, it comprised body 3422 (Series 1) and chassis 240002. Another operator that added the Mace to their fleet was sister company Southern National who had nine delivered in December in 1934. (*ECW*)

Western Welsh 720(CBO105) was one of many bodies ordered in the late 1930s for mounting on Leyland TS8 chassis. Completed at the factory in late 1939, the chassis was 303947 and body 6697 (Series 1) in B35F format. The streamline markings may indicate a coach, but official records show that these were classed as buses. (*ECW*)

Western Welsh 617(CKG797) was one of an order for fifteen bodies for delivery in 1940, seven of these were highbridge bodies and the others lowbridge. The evacuation of the Lowestoft factory restricted the construction of the bodies and only two were completed, the remaining thirteen being completed in 1946. The final lowbridge bus was 617(CKG797) which is seen here. (*ECW*)

PART TWO - FROM 1940 TO CLOSURE

By late 1940, the threat of invasion was much reduced and ECW was allowed to reopen on a limited scale their Lowestoft factory with a maximum of eight vehicles being allowed on site at any one time, a figure that was increased in 1943 to 30. Some of the buildings and parts of the site were in use by the military and this reduced the capability for any large work programme. During this difficult time, Mr. Bramham was General Manager and Works Manager. Responsibilities from 1941 at Lowestoft were undertaken by Mr. McCall. Other managerial posts at Lowestoft included Freddie Thompson (administration) and Ted Godley (production and workforce). The authorities carefully monitored the work being carried out at the factory, but many new bodies were constructed there including B35R bodies 6876- 6920 (Series 1), for Eastern Counties in 1942, mounted on Bristol L5G chassis. Other work included repairing war damaged bodies and rebodying older vehicles.

During the time that the invasion scare was greatest, the government had limited the supply of chassis and component parts and severely restricted issue of these to industry for civilian use. Once the scare had subsided, the restriction was partially lifted and ECW was allowed to undertake limited restocking of their stores and were supplied with a few Bristol chassis. It is true that when the invasion scare receded, some of the workforce were re-employed at Lowestoft, but by March 1945, there were still less than 200 employees there. During late 1944, all restrictions were lifted on both the Lowestoft and Irthlingborough factories. With the war coming to an end, the Company made a determined effort to commence rebuilding ECW to pre-war standards and build up production to something like that before the conflict. By June 1945, almost all of those who had been working at Irthlingborough had returned to Lowestoft and over the next three years the workforce was increased substantially through recruitment, with many former employees eager to get back to their old workplace. The plant, tools and machinery moved to Irthlingborough in 1940 was safely delivered back in good condition to Eastern Way.

During 1942, the TBAT group was divided up due to differences in aspects of planning and policy within the higher management of Tilling and BET. ECW was part of the TBAT group because it was a subsidiary of ECOC and the outcome of this split was that ECW was destined to be part of the Tilling empire, led by Sir Frederick Heaton, head of Thomas Tilling Ltd. Traditionally ECW had undertaken much more work for Tilling operators than those in the BET group. Some of the operators within the old TBAT group were taken by Tilling, whilst others went to BET. Two changes in the ECW board of directors had occurred in 1943 when two of the directors, Messrs. Romer and Bramham left on secondment to take up positions with Short Bros. Their replacements were Mr. Bill Shirley and Mr. Ralph Sugden both as deputy general managers. Mr. Shirley was given responsibility for production and Mr. Sugden looked after commercial activities. Also in 1943, the first prototype of the new 56 seat standard highbridge double deck body was completed and delivered to Western National. A second prototype was completed with a 55 seat lowbridge body and delivered to Eastern National in early 1944; both buses used slightly modified Bristol K5G chassis. The lowbridge, which is featured elsewhere in this book, has been preserved and is now in the fleet of the Eastern National Preservation Group. Other new double deck bodies built between 1943 and 1945 included a number for Brighton, Hove and District. These 56 seat highbridge bodies were fitted to AEC Regent chassis dating from the 1930s, and had many features of the new ECW standard highbridge body.

The ECW facility at Irthlingborough was kept fully occupied for several years building new vehicle bodies, mainly on Bristol L type chassis, for operators such as Crosville, United Automobile Services and United Counties. Rebodying and repair work on both single and double deck buses was also carried out there. The great majority of those who moved there in 1940 had returned to Lowestoft by 1945, and thereafter the work was carried out by local employees assisted by a few Lowestoft men. This facility closed in 1951 and the property was disposed of.

The end of the war in Europe on 8th May 1945 brought a large demand nationally for new public transport vehicles and by 1947 production at Lowestoft was almost back to pre-war levels, despite a general shortage of new chassis and some materials. A large number of orders were received by ECW one of which, for bodywork on nine 56 seat highbridge double deck buses with AEC Regent II chassis, came from Lowestoft Corporation. These were to be delivered a few hundreds yards down the road to the Corporation depot. In 1946, the ECW body numbering scheme, inherited from United days and known to many as Series I, was replaced by a new series of numbers known as Series 2, which started at 1001. For many years at the factory a common numbering series had been used and these covered a wide variety of work including miscellaneous jobs.

Right - United BLO223 (HHN223) was one of the two prototypes to carry the new post war single deck body design in 1946. This was completed as a bus and the other prototype, Crosville KB1 (FFM469), was completed as an express coach. BLO223 had a Bristol L5G chassis and the Crosville example had a Bristol L6A chassis. The Cromer destination blinds seen here were for demonstration purposes only. (ECW)

Below - The interior of BLO223 (ECW)

By the end of 1946, well over 5000 vehicle bodies had been constructed by United, Eastern Counties Omnibus Company and Eastern Coach Works for at least 35 different operators around the UK and overseas. In 1951 a separate numbering for repairs was introduced with the letter "R" incorporated in the number series, the first number being R501. Some other numbering schemes were used at the factory including one used to signify an experimental body or project. This series of numbers was prefixed "EX" and started at EX1. In arranging the work programme, vehicle bodies of the same type and specification were arranged in batches and the materials and parts were assembled ready for when work commenced on building the bodies in the batch. This was an efficient and cost effective way of making and ordering items required to build a number of bodies being built to the same specification and ensured continuous work flow on bodies of the same type in a batch during a given period. Thirty bodies might be a typical batch but this number would vary depending on many factors including the number of bodies ordered by operators in a certain period, and any individual differences. It could happen that an odd vehicle body was added to a batch after the initial number of bodies had been assigned a batch number. Included in this book is a copy of the document giving details of Batch 716, issued on 14th October 1986. This historic document gives details of the very last bus bodies made at ECW.

The first years after the end of Second World War saw a policy evolve of building a limited number of standard body designs at ECW, by then totally under Tilling control. For the majority of these vehicles the chassis used would be those manufactured by Bristol, another part of the Tilling group. Tilling favoured this cost effective standardisation approach to work practices which had proven to be very productive and a way of driving out inefficiency. This policy even extended to the livery applied to vehicles operated by Tilling group operators, this generally being red or green. Other operators continued to have more individual body work supplied by ECW including BET companies and some municipals. The different coloured liveries on these vehicles were in pleasant contrast to the standard colours of the Tilling group vehicles and made a colourful sight especially in and around Lowestoft, when they were undertaking road tests, visiting one of the two weighbridges in the town used by ECW, or leaving the town on delivery to the new owner.

Unsettling news came in 1948 that would lead to another change in the ownership of ECW and also Bristol. A far reaching change in the company's position followed the voluntary nationalisation of the Tilling group in 1948-49 whereupon the bus interests passed to the British Transport Commission (BTC). This had been set up by the Labour Government to run much of the nation's road, rail and sea transport network under state ownership and meant that ECW and Bristol were no longer allowed to produce vehicles for operators other than those controlled by the BTC, although any outstanding work for non BTC operators was completed, the last being in 1950. Some of these non BTC operators had large coach and bus fleets and had been good, sincere customers over many years. One positive aspect of the nationalisation was that ECW was able to plan for large scale production of standardised vehicles for the many nationalised bus fleets across the UK.

The period between the end of World War Two and the early 1950s saw the completion of a great number of bodies on the well proven and popular Bristol K series double deck chassis and the L series single deck chassis, both of which dated from the late 1930s. A number of variations in the basic standard designs for both double deck and single deck chassis were developed including a coach and dual purpose body for the single deck chassis. As well as those already mentioned, ECW built bodies for a wide variety of operators in the post war years including Aberdare, Merthyr Tydfil, East Kent, East Yorkshire, Ribble, North Western, Tynemouth, Northern General, Southdown, Birch Bros., Ebor Bus Co., and Red & White. The bodies built for Aberdare Council were unusual in that wooden slatted seating was specified for the vehicles, the chassis of which were Bristol L6As. It was reported that the reason for this was that the clothes of coal miners would have soon dirtied the upholstery and seat fabric.

With many double deck bodies and the equivalent single deck bodies being constructed at the factory and until 1951, at Irthlingborough, ECW was working at full capacity in the late 1940s and early 1950s. An interesting export order for 50 single deck metal bodied buses on Bristol LWL6G chassis was completed in 1948 for South Africa. The majority of these buses seated 39 passengers but five were built to cater for 46. Unfortunately due to restrictions imposed on ECW when it was nationalised, this promising order could not be followed up and a wonderful opportunity was lost. The Bristol LWL chassis was wider and longer than the normal Bristol L chassis and in 1948 could not be used in the UK due to various restrictions on the length and width of bus and coach bodies. Whilst wide bodies could be up to 8ft. in 1948, there were restrictions on where a vehicle that width could travel. Changes in the regulations regarding the maximum length of public service vehicles (PSV) came in 1950 when the maximum permissible length of a single decker was increased from 27ft. 6ins. to 30ft., and that for a double decker with two axles, from 26ft. to 27ft. The restrictions on where an 8ft. wide PSV could travel were relaxed. Further changes came in 1956 when the maximum permissible length for two axle double deckers was increased to 30ft. and in 1962 when the maximum length of a single decker was increased to 36ft. An increase in the regulation width of PSVs was also amended at this time to 8ft. 2½ins. Other unusual body work completed during 1948 included four 35 seat single deck buses for the Londonderry and Lough Swilly Railway with AEC Regal III chassis, fifteen double deck bodies for East Yorkshire with the unique "Beverley" roof and twenty-five 55 five seat double deck bodies for Red & White with Albion Venturer chassis.

Both London Transport and ECW were now under BTC control and in 1948 with a serious shortage of buses in London, it was arranged that some new double deck buses being built by ECW for a variety of operators, were to be loaned to London Transport. Over 200 buses were involved in this temporary loan comprising vehicles that were intended for Brighton Hove & District, Crosville, Eastern Counties and Hants & Dorset. The loans lasted for two years and the buses involved were all Bristol K series consisting of both lowbridge and highbridge designs. The designs of bodies being built at ECW in the late 1940s had been basically unchanged since the end of the Second World War but this was soon to change.

A fine example of combined research and development by Bristol and ECW resulted in the Bristol Lodekka, no doubt one of the best known British double deck buses. This revolutionary new design of front engined low height double deck bus appeared in prototype form in 1949 and, after a small number of pre-production buses had been built and assessed, it entered production with modifications in 1953.

In 1946, Crosville MB251 (FFW432) had the distinction of having a body that had been given the first number in the second series of body numbers used at the factory. This 55 seat bus had a Bristol K6A chassis.
(ECW)

The Bristol Lodekka was a truly great British design and became one of the best known buses of all time. Mansfield & District 545 (241MNN) comprised chassis FLF6G 199.139 with body 13168 and was completed in October 1962. Many Lodekkas survive in different parts of the world although this particular bus is not one of them, (ECW)

The Lodekka obviated the need for the unpopular off set sunken side gangway on the upper deck of double deck buses, where overall height was constrained by low bridges by using a low chassis frame and a dropped-centre double-reduction rear axle. Initially the Lodekka had a sunken central gangway on the lower deck but in 1958 it was announced that as part of a package of improvements for the Lodekka it would in future have a virtually flat lower deck floor as well as a flat upper deck. Early versions had a rear entrance but later models had a front entrance with platform or sliding doors available. The robust and reliable Lodekka family was a major success and had many variants. Designations used to identify different types of Lodekka included LD, LDL, LFL, LFS, FS, FL, FSF and FLF. By the time production ceased in 1968, over 5200 examples had been built at Lowestoft, some of which can still be found throughout the world since many were sold and exported after disposal by operators in the UK.

A unique body was designed and manufactured at ECW in 1950 that used mechanical parts originating from withdrawn Dennis Ace buses to produce 16 chassisless single deck buses for ECOC. Of half cab layout, the 32 seat buses were rear entrance and had radiators specially designed at the factory. After completion of this order no further examples were built. This design was followed in 1951 by another for mounting on an AEC Regal IV underfloor engined chassis. This body was intended for dual use and could seat 39 passengers. Twenty were built, with fifteen going to London Transport and the other five to Tilling. Another new design this time for a coach was unveiled in 1950 and, unusually, was not based on an ECW bus body design. Until then the majority of coach bodies had been derived from bus bodies. The 27ft. 6ins. full fronted cab design was for mounting on the Bristol L6B chassis and had the most appealing clean styling. The following year a 30ft. version of the coach mounted on the larger Bristol LWL6B chassis was unveiled. One of the main differences to the earlier model was that the front had been radically altered with the radiator now placed behind an attractive grill. The 1950 design had 31 seats and the later larger coach had 35 seats with greater leg room. There were several examples of this type of body being used on other chassis including those of AEC and Leyland manufacture. Unexpectedly, a further 10 bodies of similar design to those built in 1951 were ordered by United Automobile Services for delivery in 1957. These were bodies

9993-10003 configured to B39C on Bristol LL5G chassis. Body 10002 was not built. These buses were intended for use on summer services around the attractive North and South Bays at Scarborough. The well supported ECW Sports & Social Club at one time operated a coach with a similar body to the 1951 design. Needless to say this was well cared for at the factory!
Two special orders were received by ECW for delivery in 1952 and 1953. The first was from British Road Services to provide 50 cabs and flat platform bodies for use on Bristol HG6L chassis. A further order for 39 was dealt with by Irthlingborough.
The second special order was from London Transport for 84 twenty six seat bodies on Guy chassis. Classified by London Transport as the Guy Special (GS), these very attractive little buses were powered by a Perkins P6 diesel engine. The last of the Guy Specials was withdrawn from service in March 1972, and many have passed into preservation.

Another example of good teamwork by Bristol and ECW was the development of the Light Saloon or LS, an underfloor engined single deck vehicle in which the body formed an integral part of the complete vehicle. The first prototype appeared in December 1950, with the second following a few months later. They were designed to accommodate four different engines, the Gardner 4HLW, 5HLW and 6HLW, and the Bristol LSW, each of which were developed from the corresponding vertical unit. The opportunity was taken to reduce the overall weight of the vehicle wherever possible but not to the extent whereby it would be considered flimsy. The LS chassis was used for both coach and bus applications. It was in production from 1951 until 1958, by which time 1392 examples had been completed. Both prototypes and over 20 production models have been preserved.

The Bristol L series single deck, half-cab, bus body was at the end of a long and successful production run when the last six bodies, 8427-32 of B39R configuration, were built to a special order for delivery in 1955. Three were for Southern National and the other three for Western National. The main production had ceased in 1952, when a fine replacement, the LS became widely available. With the Bristol Lodekka firmly established in many bus fleets in the UK as the standard double deck bus, time was running out for the well proven and familiar Bristol K series. The last of these distinctive double deck bus bodies were completed during 1957 with Brighton Hove & District, Bristol Omnibus and Cheltenham and District being the last operators supplied with bodywork for these reliable sturdy vehicles. The last one was Bristol Omnibus No. C8431 (YHT927) a KSW6G with chassis 118.037 and body 9656 and like all those delivered to Bristol in 1957, was of H33/27R configuration. A new design building on the considerable success of the Bristol LS was unveiled in 1957 when the first of the seven prototype Medium Weight or MW single deckers was completed. The body was intended for use as a bus, coach or dual purpose. With production of the LS coming to an end in 1958, it was essential that the MW was in production as soon as possible

after the launch and during 1957, 140 were completed by ECW. As with other ECW designs, the MW could be adapted for use with other chassis. In the case of the LS, a similar body was used by ECW on a number of Leyland Royal Tiger chassis for orders placed by United Automobile Services in 1952/3. In 1961 a much more flamboyant MW coach body design, having little resemblance to the original, was introduced. In total at least 23 operators had versions of the extremely successful MW in their fleets with United Automobile Services, Crosville, Red & White and Bristol Omnibus all having at least 200. After over 1900 MW bodies had been completed, production ended in 1967.

The Bristol LS was in production from 1951 until 1958 and over 1400 were built. United had a total of 328 Bristol LS series vehicles comprising buses, dual purpose use and coaches. United BU91 (VHN891) was completed in December 1954 with body 7478 configured as B45F. This bus had a Bristol LS5G chassis, the most common type. (ECW)

At least 80 examples of this joint Bristol/ECW venture been preserved with a great many of these superbly restored, and in roadworthy condition.

A fair amount of rebodying and refurbishment work was part of the ongoing work at ECW, in addition to many small orders from operators for non standard work which was not considered as part of the main work programme. During 1954, a new model known as the Bristol Small Capacity or SC appeared. Intended for use as a bus or coach, production ran from 1954 until 1962 with over 320 bodies being built. Some of the first completed went to Eastern National but other operators such as Crosville, Lincolnshire and Eastern Counties soon ordered these cost effective vehicles that were ideal for the less busy routes and where one man operation was economically necessary. One interesting fact concerning the SC is that two bodies, EX5 and 11981 were made entirely of glass fibre at ECW in 1960. These were fitted to chassis SC4LK147.050 and SC4LK158.035 and later EX5 became ECOC LC565 and 11981 became Crosville SSG664. A casual glance at these buses would have given the impression they were of normal construction. Neither exists today.

A considerable number of Bristol L series half cab vehicles were rebuilt in 1958 with SC type bodies for Southern National, Thames Valley and Western National. These buses, built to FB39F configuration, had their chassis extended to accommodate the replacement body. The SC has been a popular choice for the preservationists with at least eighteen known to be preserved.

Production during the period 1955 - 57 included bodywork for vehicles with AEC Regent 111, Bristol K series, L series, Lodekka (LD), LS, MW and SC and Guy Arab 11 chassis. Bodywork was also completed in 1957 on one very notable double deck coach. A Routemaster was built to London Transport's own specification with body 8250 to CH32/25RD configuration. Hopes of a large order for these vehicles came to nothing and it was the only such vehicle ever built at ECW. It was intended for operation on Green Line services.

ECW had a reputation that it could build bodies for anything on wheels and in 1958 an order for two 56 seat diesel railbuses from British Railways went some way to proving this. The underframes for the railbuses were manufactured by Bristol Commercial Vehicles at Brislington and fitted with Gardner 112hp engines.

Testing of the underframes was carried out late at night between Brislington station and Pensford with temporary cabs fitted at each end of the underframes for protection. The underframes had been taken the short distance from the factory to the station by road. After testing, they were conveyed to Lowestoft by BRS (Pickfords) Ltd., where the already assembled 42ft. 7ins. long bodies were fitted. In order to deliver the completed railbuses to British Railways, a temporary track was laid from the factory to the nearby Great Yarmouth - Lowestoft railway line. The railbuses, SC79958 and SC79959, spent most of their lives working in Scotland. A further order from British Railways for delivery in 1959 was for a "go anywhere" mobile test laboratory mounted on a Bedford 4 wheel drive chassis. The vehicle was needed to gain access from the road across rough ground to parts of the railway infrastructure such as bridges, tunnels and viaducts. When completed the Bedford resembled hundreds of British Army lorries that had a similar chassis. Completed with body 10086 (215HRO), the British Railways serial number was 1033S. Further details of this vehicle can be found on Page 48.

Late 1959 saw the launch of another joint venture between ECW and Bristol when the Bristol SU (Small Underfloor) was unveiled. The SU was intended to replace the SC and was produced between 1960 and 1966 in two lengths, the SUL at around 28ft. seated 36 passengers as a bus and 33 as a coach, and the SUS at 24ft. 4ins. seated 30 passengers. Both models were 7ft. 6ins. wide. Powered by an Albion EN250H 4 cylinder 4.1 Litre engine with a five speed David Brown gearbox the SU was ideal for rural services. There were 181 Bristol SU's built; 25 SUS buses and 156 SUL made up of 118 buses and 38 coaches. The SU was operated by Western National (83), Southern National (50), West Yorkshire (18), Bristol Omnibus (9), Southern Vectis (8), United Counties (6), United Automobiles (5) and United Welsh (2). Production ceased in 1966 when a replacement lightweight vehicle was planned.

By the early 1960s, the workforce numbered just over 1,100 and the output of new vehicles was in the region of 700 per annum. At that time, Eastern Coach Works was considered to be one of the most up to date and best equipped bus and coach building factories in the country and the company's products were renowned for their high standard of build. A gradual changeover

from the use of timber to metal had been made in the post war period with aluminium alloys being used extensively in body construction. The change from timber to metal construction necessitated a certain amount of re-equipping and the installation of new machinery. However, men formerly employed in the machining and assembly of timber parts quickly adapted themselves to the handling of aluminium alloys and in some cases the machines that previously cut and shaped timber parts were adapted to the forming and manipulation of metal parts.
No industrial concern can afford to lag behind in development and research and Eastern Coach Works was no exception. New materials and methods of manufacture called for constant investigation into the possibility of their application to the fine products built at the Lowestoft factory. Full time staff were engaged in research and development work and these people occupied a large separate department for this purpose. A team of some 16 qualified draughtsmen kept the production shops supplied with drawings, material schedules and general information relating to the work in hand and the team spirit throughout the works was very largely responsible for the smooth flow of output.

During 1962, Bristol introduced a versatile rear engined single deck chassis known as the Rear Engine or RE. Three lengths were available these being 32ft. 6ins. for the RES, 36ft. for the REL and or 39ft. for the REM with the chassis being bodied for use as a bus, coach or dual purpose. All lengths of chassis were supplied in low or high-framed versions, the low-framed for bus work and the high-framed for coach and express work giving the type codes as RELL, RELH, RESL etc. The chassis of the RELL and RESL was ramped upwards from the front, allowing a shallow entrance, whereas the RELH chassis was almost level, giving a higher floor, mainly used for coaches. This range of chassis eventually became very popular with operators of all kinds including many municipal operators and some independents. The bodywork produced by ECW was continually refined and updated throughout the production run leading to a good looking, reliable, quality single deck vehicle. Everybody liked the superb RE except apparently Leyland, who in later years may have seen it as being a threat and in the way when it came to selling their new Leyland National. In the 21st century the RE design does not look out of place alongside new vehicles built to the latest EU standards and certainly has a more refined and dignified character. Production of the RE body ran until July 1975 with some of the last being RESL B47F bodies for Merseyside PTE and RELL B46D bodies built for Hartlepool Corporation Transport. The period 1960-64 was a very busy time for ECW with hundreds of bodies being ordered by a wide selection of operators for use with many types of chassis that included :- AEC Regal IV, Bristol FL6B, FL6G, FLF6B, FLF6G, FLF6L, FS5G, FS6B, FS6G, FSF6B, FSF6G, L5G, LD6B, LD6G, LL5G, LL6A, LL6B, MW5G, MW6G, RELH6B, RELH6G, RELL6G, SC4LK, SUL4A, SUS4A and Leyland L1.

The bodywork of the Bristol MW underwent several changes during the production run of this popular type. Hants & Dorset 897(AEL5B) was new in May 1964 and had 3 other owners during its life. The chassis was 213.173 and the body 14468 configured to C39F. (*ECW*)

The Bristol RE range of buses and coaches was very successful. Completed in June 1971 with B40D bodywork, Aldershot & District 644 (YHO635J) was an RESL6G with body 19544. (*ECW*)

Bedford was an unusual chassis manufacturer in the 1960s for ECW to work with but, with the introduction of the Vauxhall Motors VAM bus chassis in the summer of 1965, ECW set about modifying their standard 45 seat bus body for mounting on it. Seen as a stop gap before the availability of the versatile Bristol LH, one of the operators to buy the VAM was Western National.

The British Transport Commission was succeeded in 1963 by the Transport Holding Company; however this new controlling body initially made little impact on the daily events at the ECW and, by the mid 1960s, Eastern Coach Works employed approximately 1,200 people. All of these were housed in one group of buildings on the original site and output of new vehicle bodies was averaging around 720 per annum. In mid 1965, it was announced by a Government spokesman that an agreement had been reached whereby Leyland Motors would acquire a 25% stake in ECW and Bristol. The immediate effect of this change in ownership was that ECW could again accept orders from other than nationalised operators and also submit tenders for bodywork on chassis made by different manufacturers including Leyland and Daimler, a freedom that had been taken away from ECW in 1948.

The mid 1960s were a period of change in the bus industry generally and at the ECW a number of single and double deck vehicles that had been the mainstay of production for a number of years, including the much acclaimed Lodekka and the award winning Medium Weight (MW), were being phased out to make way for new models. The MW body design was used in a number of different applications from stage carriage work to long distance express, touring or limited stop work and was adapted for use on a number of different chassis, including those of other manufacturers. The recognised replacement was the RE rear-engined single-decker, a vehicle already receiving good sales and great interest across the UK.

The Lodekka was succeeded by the Bristol VR, a rear-engined double deck vehicle that was destined to have a long production run at ECW from 1968 to 1981. As with the Lodekka, this became a familiar sight on the roads of much of the UK whilst serving with many operators. The first prototypes were exhibited at the Commercial Motor Show at Earls Court in September 1966. The first prototype, VRX001, was in Central SMT livery on display at the ECW stand, and the second, VRX002, in Bristol Omnibus Company livery at the BCV stand. Powered by 10.45 litre Gard-

ner 6LX engines they were 32ft. 7ins. long, 13ft. 8ins. high and 8ft. 2½ ins. wide. They seated 45 passengers on the upper deck and 35 on the lower and the bodywork was semi-integral with the chassis. An electrically operated door was fitted and positioned forward of the front axle and the right hand spiral staircase was situated behind the driver. The engine was mounted vertically at the rear offside corner of the vehicle with access from an exterior detachable side panel and rear offside hinged fibreglass corner panel. Externally much of the bodywork design was derived from the Lodekka, but with a redesigned and almost vertical front and rear. Using a highbridge internal layout, the Bristol VRX was of normal lowbridge height with the engine very cleverly concealed. VRX001 and 002 were extensively tested and used in service by a number of operators, the resulting weaknesses in the design were rectified and the VRL as it became, was ready for full scale production. Both Bristol and ECW wanted the new design to be a worthy successor to the tremendously successful Lodekka.

The first production Leyland engined VRL was completed in late 1968 and in total 30 double deck coaches, with VRLLH6L chassis and ECW bodywork, were built and successfully operated by Standerwick, a Ribble subsidiary. Three of the thirty are known still to exist, one of which is operational in Geelong, Victoria, Australia. At the 1968 Commercial Motor Show, the Standerwick coach proved to be an impressive and popular exhibit. These 60 seat 36ft. coaches were used on motorway express services and had many additional features including a large luggage area and toilets. Due to government policy regarding grants, new vehicles and one man operation, the VRL was not suitable for the changing mass bus market and needed some redesign work to be carried out prior to relaunch as a major bus fleet vehicle. One major change in the new redesigned VR to the VRL was the positioning of the engine; this was transversely mounted across the rear instead of the offside rear.

The result of the changes and modifications produced a vehicle that became a major success for Bristol across the UK with thousands of the redesigned VRs, known as the VRT, being built with ECW providing the great majority of the bodies. The last coach with a VRLLH6L chassis was delivered in August 1972 with body 19854, and with that production of the VRL ceased. ECW built bodies for over 3,800 vehicles of the VR range consisting of VRX, VRLLH, VRTLL, VRTSL and VRTLH designs. By far the largest number of bodies built by ECW was for the VRTSL, which were up to 30ft. 9ins. long. The height of the standard body was 13ft. 8ins. and the full height body was 14ft 6ins. An ultra low body was also available. While the great majority of double deck bodies built in the mid 1970s at the factory were for the Bristol VRT, bodywork of a similar design was constructed for fitting to other rear engined double deck chassis around that time. Large numbers of Leyland Atlanteans were completed at Eastern Way for operators such as Ribble, Northern General, East Kent, Trent and Midland General while other operators including South Yorkshire PTE, Colchester Borough Transport and Thamesdown, were supplied with bodywork for their Daimler Fleetlines. Although their numbers are rapidly dwindling, in 2007 some late Bristol VR buses with ECW bodywork are still licensed and at work mainly on school, charter and special duties.

These well designed vehicles never seemed to age, however first hand experience as a passenger travelling 62 miles each working day in one, could well result in a different opinion.

The author travelled well over 36,000 miles in Bristol VR double deck buses operated by ECOC in the late 1980s and early 1990s on the X74 Lowestoft - Norwich service. He witnessed many times water seeping through the floor on the lower deck of numerous vehicles whenever the roads were wet and experienced the total lack of heating; with two occasions when ice formed on the inside of the bus windows. The wet floor and the cold in winter were not good advertisements for the VRT and in the 21st century would not be tolerated for this length of journey. Other experiences included two engine failures in the depths of winter in the Norfolk countryside requiring on each occasion a spare bus (another VRT) to be sent out from the Lowestoft garage to rescue the stranded passengers. One of the failures was during a blizzard near Loddon with drifting snow and slush everywhere but we eventually got to Norwich in the spare bus. Fortunately, on each occasion a regular passenger had a large early analogue mobile telephone which the driver used to call for help. The driver apologised to the passengers and explained that a great deal was being expected from the old buses that were used on the X74 service and they were getting past their "sell by date". All most passengers wanted was just to get to work on time. You needed to be a true bus lover to endure such winter conditions for a journey lasting 1½ hours or longer in winter if the traffic into Norwich was heavy.

However, one day a newly refurbished Series Three VRT turned up at Lowestoft Bus Station to work the X74 service. With new clean seats, new floor coverings, a reconditioned door and new paintwork the bus looked almost new and to crown it all this one, quite unbelievably had just had heating installed! After a week working the X74, this fine VR with no leaky floor disappeared and it was back to normal on the Lowestoft to Norwich run with the leaky cold vehicles.

The second prototype Bristol VR (or N type), HHW966D demonstrates the long rear overhang necessary to accommodate the length of the longitudinal engine. The body was EX11.(*ECW*)

New in June 1978, VJA665S comprised chassis VRT/SL3/6LXB/1327 and body 23452. This was one of three Bristol VRTs with H41/29F bodywork supplied to A. Mayne & Sons of Manchester. This standard 13ft. 8ins. bus was broken up for spares in 2002. (*ECW*)

Why were the VRs used on this popular limited stop service in such a run down condition? Although it was unusual to see this bus on the service, the best local VR used on the X74 at that time was ECOC VR385, now preserved at the Transport Museum at Carlton Colville. A surprise one cold wet dark winter morning at Lowestoft Bus Station was the arrival of a very smart blue ECW bodied AEC Swift single deck bus belonging to Gt. Yarmouth Corporation. This was a replacement for the Bristol VR that would normally work the heavily loaded X74 service. According to the driver all the Lowestoft based VRs were out of service for various reasons and being short of serviceable buses the Corporation Transport Department at Yarmouth was helping out by supplying vehicles to ECOC. By the time the Swift got to Norwich it resembled a London underground tube train in the rush hour. Nobody checked the number of passengers on board and the driver gave up collecting fares due to the chaotic and overcrowded conditions. The joys of daily commuting by bus!

A neat single deck design with some features of the body used for the RE chassis was unveiled by ECW in 1967 on a Bristol LH chassis. The LH (Light Horizontal) was an ideal choice for one man operation and use on services where a smaller vehicle was sufficient. It was built in two lengths, the LHS being a shorter version of the LH and was the final single deck chassis to be designed by BCV. Like several other ECW bodies including that used on the VRT, the LH was initially fitted with a flat windscreen. The design of the front was changed in 1968 and again in 1972 when one of the alterations was the introduction of a curved windscreen. Engine types available with the LH were those of Perkins or Leyland manufacture. The LH was very successful and sold in large numbers to many operators including London Transport. The final LH bodies built at Eastern Way were for National Welsh, Western National, Southern Vectis and Ribble with the last three bodies, configured as DP27F for National Welsh leaving the factory in February 1981 as their MD9025/6/8. Those for Ribble and Western National were configured as B35F and Southern Vectis as DP31F, these left the factory between October 1980 and January 1981. The last LHS with ECW bodywork was built for National Welsh and completed in September 1981. It was body 25064, configured as B35F and became in their fleet MD8116 (KWO570X). An LH was displayed at the 1968 Commercial Motor Show in full ECOC livery. The end of production of the LH marked the end of large scale manufacture of small bus bodies at ECW. Many LH buses with ECW bodywork exist today in service and in preservation.

In the late 1960s, with a workforce of over 1,000, the output at ECW was running at 15 bodies per week; the factory was as busy as ever with seemingly a very prosperous future. A further exhibit at the 1968 Commercial Motor Show, but on the AEC stand, was a luxury coach with bodywork by ECW. The body had been supplied for an AEC Sabre chassis and the vehicle on display was the end result. A much heard comment regarding this coach was "which is the front and which is the back". Unusually for a vehicle with ECW designed bodywork the coach never entered production, the AEC chassis and the large 247hp engine failing to attract orders. One positive outcome of the Sabre body design was that some elements could be used in future coach bodywork.

Further news regarding the ongoing saga of the ownership of ECW was forthcoming in July 1969 when Leyland Motors, by then renamed British Leyland, increased their shareholding in ECW and also Bristol to 50%, the remaining 50% being retained by the newly formed National Bus Company. Around that same time a new company, Leyland National Ltd., was formed as a joint venture by British Leyland and the National Bus Company to build buses at a new factory in Workington in Cumberland. Within a few years this venture would have serious repercussions for Bristol and ECW since the establishment of this large mass production unit by Leyland would lead to the end of large scale single deck bus body production at Lowestoft including the highly rated and popular RE, and would eventually affect the viability of the complete Lowestoft operation. Those in the industry had to reconsider their future options since the new plant would affect all the British bus manufacturing businesses.

Unexpected management changes occurred in 1970 as a result of the sudden death of Ralph Sugden following a heart attack. His position as General Manager was filled by Alf Tattersall and Syd Wright became the Works Manager. Little change was seen at the factory as a result of these moves, but before long there would be changes as Leyland started to bring ECW in line with their ways.

City of Oxford Motor Services 71 (GBW71L) was a forty nine seat coach with body 19878 and chassis RELH-4-484. It was powered by a six cylinder Gardner engine and one of 57 similar vehicles bodied in the last half of 1972 for a number of operators. (ECW)

Great Yarmouth Borough Transport placed orders with United, ECOC and ECW over several years and continued in 1972 with an order for B43D bodywork on 12 AEC Swift 3MP2R chassis. Great Yarmouth 82 (WEX682M) with body 20830, is seen here in October 1972. (ECW)

Ipswich Borough Transport 73 (LDX73G) was one of four H43/31F bodies completed in November 1968 on Leyland Atlantean chassis. No. 73 was fitted with body 17198 and had chassis PDR1/1 802807. (ECW)

Several demonstration vehicles with ECW bodies were sent to different countries in the hope of winning orders. Seen here in Alexandria, Egypt, undergoing evaluation trials this Olympian is about to pass a donkey and cart. It had entered service there in April 1984. (Leyland)

A new 49 seat coach body design was introduced in 1972 intended for mounting on the Leyland Leonard and Bristol RELH chassis. The new design had clean straight lines, flat sides, four large panoramic windows with fixed glazing and in some ways resembled a Plaxton or Duple bodied coach. The design remained in production with a small adjustment in the overall length until 1975. Several operators were supplied with this body including Alder Valley, Crosville, Northern General, Oxford, South Midland, Ribble, SELNEC PTE and Trent. The future of this design was influenced by the arrival on the scene of the Leyland National and it was not promoted as much as it could have been.

The period 1971-75 saw a large number of operators ordering over 2,000 bodies for mounting on chassis that included :-

AEC SW 3MP2R, Bristol LH6L, LH6P, LHS6L, RELH6G, RELH6L, RELL6G, RELL6L, RESL6G, RESL6L, VRLLH6L, VRTSL6G (Series 2), VRTSL6G (Series 3), VRTSL6LX (Series 3), VRTSL6LXB (Series 3), VRTSL501 (Series 3), Daimler CRG6, CRL6, CRG6LX, CRG6LXB, Leyland AN68/1R, FE30AGR, PDR1A/1, PSU3B/4R, PSU3C/4R.

During 1981, a new coach body design coded B51 was unveiled. This was intended for use with the Bristol RELH chassis and as a trial an Eastern National RELH6G, body 19857, was rebuilt to the new design. ECOC was one of the first to be interested in a re-bodying exercise and nominated five RELH chassis to have new bodies fitted since the trial vehicle with the new body was hailed as a considerable success. The original plans were modified when Leyland decided that a better idea was to use new Leyland Leopard chassis which they had available.
Production of altered bodies started at ECW with these intended for mounting on the Leyland chassis instead of the Bristol RELH. Several operators ordered the body mostly in the C49F configuration including Alder Valley, Cumberland, East Kent, ECOC, Lincolnshire, Northern General, Southern Vectis, United Counties and Yorkshire Traction. Similar bodies were also supplied for use on the Leyland Tiger chassis of which London County was a major user. A modified body design was used on the longer Leyland chassis and these seated between 50 and 57 passengers. Unusually for an ECW design, problems arose when structural failures

appeared in the body of these coaches and modification kits had to be produced at the factory. These were either sent to operators for fitting to the coach bodies or they were fitted by ECW staff at the operators premises. The feeling was that rather than ECW being at fault, the domineering Leyland policy had caused the problem. The excellent relationship that had existed for many years between BCV and ECW where each party considered the other on an equal footing had prevented such happenings in the past. With Leyland it was different.

During November 1982, it was announced that the National Bus Company had disposed of its interests in Bus Manufacturers (Holdings) Ltd. to Leyland. For the first time, British Leyland had complete control of ECW, Bristol Commercial Vehicles, Leyland National and others including bus manufacturer C. H. Roe. The ownership of the relatively new factory at Workington also passed to British Leyland. The feeling was that the Workington factory would reduce the requirement for bus and coach bodies to be built at Lowestoft and chassis at Bristol. In the event, it was the fall in demand and the ending of Leyland National production that meant spare capacity was available there. It became apparent that the modern Workington factory would always get priority for any large scale work that was available especially when orders for public service vehicles were declining.

Covering an area of 14 acres, Eastern Coach Works was one of the largest coachworks in the country and despite the lack of orders and a very uncertain future, continued to turn out high quality work. The loss of a £3million expansion programme and a possible 300 additional jobs in 1980 when management and unions failed to agree on production terms and conditions for a new type of double deck bus, the Leyland Titan, damaged the long term future of the factory and the workforce. The media called this event one of the saddest chapters in the history of Eastern Coach Works. By 1983, output was down to just 5 bodies per week and with a lack of orders for ECW it was very difficult to foresee how the factory could continue, but it had been in a similar position in the past and had made a complete recovery. This time however, the circumstances were different and ECW found itself in a very competitive market with declining customer orders, a series of substantial job losses expected and an additional modern Leyland factory able to mass produce buses and coaches. The bus industry was shocked and surprised in January 1983, when it was announced that Bristol Commercial Vehicles, a long term partner of ECW, would close. The work carried out there including production of the new Olympian chassis, would be transferred to the Leyland plant at Workington with parts being manufactured at other Leyland sources. Designed and originally built by Bristol Commercial Vehicles, the Olympian had been officially launched in October 1980 by Bristol as the B45 chassis and was seen as a replacement for the ageing Atlantean, Fleetline and VR range of double-deck chassis. Production of the B45 chassis had begun in 1981, the same year as the very last VRT left the Lowestoft factory. At ECW in February 1983, it was announced that 98 employees out of the workforce of around 700 would be made redundant. A statement from Eastern Coach Works parent company Leyland Buses, blamed the series of job losses on the continued low demand for buses, coupled with little prospect of any major upturn in the foreseeable future and over capacity in the industry. The statement continued by saying that the Lowestoft factory had been successful in winning new customers, but these did not compensate for the dramatic downturn in the

general demand for buses and the over capacity in the UK bus manufacturing industry.

Leyland's Public Relations Manger, Mr. Trevor Longcroft, stated that no assurances could be given on the future of the company. It was hoped that the redundancies would be voluntary, and after that, a process of early retirements would be introduced with others leaving on a "last in, first out" basis. Further redundancies followed including those during the following May when another 60 jobs were lost. By the end of that month the workforce had been reduced to around 540, and these jobs were by no means considered safe.

In early May, Leyland had announced a new plant director to replace Mr. John Bloor who was due to retire that month. Mr. Bloor's replacement was 32 year old Mr. Peter Middleton, who had joined Leyland as a graduate trainee and had worked at an executive level for the Company for 8 years.

In these very difficult times for ECW at Lowestoft, Leyland Bus moved into a new office block in Thurston Road at Leyland, Lancashire during August and September 1984, something that did not go unnoticed by the Lowestoft workforce!

Ironically, in 1984 ten Leyland Titans, the bus involved in the 1980 dispute, arrived at Lowestoft. They were part of a batch of 37 London Transport buses sent to the ECW for repair and maintenance that also included 20 Routemasters and some Leyland National single deck buses. At the time of their arrival, it was reported that the factory and the remaining workforce was pleased to be involved with an organisation that ran 8000 buses every day in the capital and was hoping for further refurbishment work from London Transport. During the last few years of ECW, much speciality work was undertaken including numerous double deck coaches for operators in the UK and overseas and work on the Leyland-DAB midibus project.

London Buses Olympian C34 (C34CHM) comprising ECW body 26136 and chassis ONLXB/1RH ON2316. *(Copyright Norman Fairhead)*

Quality and robustness of construction, a long established feature of ECW products, was reinforced when at the 1984 International Motor Show a double deck luxury coach with ECW bodywork built for Kent operator Ebdon's and based on the Olympian, won the Gold Cup and the Leyland-DAB midibus won the Silver Cup. So close to closure and ECW was still the best.

Due to legal changes within Leyland, from the 1st January 1985, the workforce at the ECW became employees of Leyland Vehicles Ltd.; previously they had been employed by Bus Manufacturers Ltd. The change followed the ending of the partnership agreement between Leyland and the National Bus Company within the ownership of Bus Manufacturers Ltd., which was effectively no longer a separate entity. The employment terms and conditions for the Lowestoft workforce remained unaltered.

In 1983 Mr. Peter Middleton took over as Plant Director at ECW and despite his best efforts to keep the factory open, others had different ideas. Mr. Middleton was succeeded by Mr. Michael Sheehan.
(Leyland Times)

An extremely successful ECW open day was held on 20th July 1985 when £3,500 was raised for a CT Scanner Appeal. The event gave employees the opportunity to show their families and members of the public the work carried out at the factory. In addition to having all aspects of the factory open, a full programme of entertainment was provided with bands, sideshows and displays by a Ju-Jitsu club and the Westerners, a cowboy club. The owners of many heritage buses and coaches, all with ECW bodywork, brought their vehicles to the factory, many travelling hundreds of miles to attend this very unique event. A full range of refreshments were also available and throughout the day the factory was packed with over 10,000 people attending, Social Club Chairman Colin Baldwin was delighted with the response from employees

and the public and thanked all concerned for a magnificent effort. In a message to mark the occasion, Mr. Peter Middleton made the point that the bus and coach market had seen dramatic changes with the cessation of the Government Grant of 50% on new bus purchases and the proposed deregulation of UK bus services. These factors had resulted in a market requirement collapse from 2,400 vehicles in 1980 to a projected total of fewer than 1,000 for 1986. He stated that the ECW must look to other markets and develop quality coach products as well as seek overseas customers for orders. The company had already made good progress overseas with orders from Greece, Hong Kong CityBus and the USA. It was hoped that other orders would be forthcoming from Thailand, Saudi Arabia and Portugal. In the UK the company was supplying the National Bus Company with vehicles and also Lothian Regional Transport. He concluded by announcing that a major order from London Buses for 260 ECW Olympians had been received. Ironically five months later in December 1985, Leyland announced a further 40 redundancies at ECW.

Starting in 1984, a small but steadily growing part of the ECW output was the supply of component parts to other Leyland Bus plants. This work was obtained through an enquiry tendering system and required ECW to be competitive with outside suppliers. It was based on a fixed tender price and delivery on time. Items supplied included Leyland Titan panels, fibreglass components, trim items and wiring looms. The prospects were good for expansion in this line with many orders arriving at Workington including a large order for 50 three-carriage Railbuses for British Rail. Transport costs for the 400 mile journey north were minimal since the components were sent on the regular delivery vehicles that came from the northern plants to Lowestoft with chassis and would otherwise return empty.

Export sales saw Hong Kong Citybus take delivery of three luxury tri-axle 77 seat coaches in 1985 for use between Hong Kong and Guandong province in China. Previous to this order, the Kowloon Bus Company had been supplied with tri-axle double deck buses based on the Olympian chassis. The order from Greece was for 20 ECW bodied Olympians adapted for use on Athens crowded city streets. Prior to receiving the order, an Olympian undertook trials in the city and at one point was loaded with 120 passengers.

At ECW in 1985 the installation of the former C. A. Roe bus building paint plant was underway with completion intended for May. For the first time in its history ECW was able to spray paint buses and coaches. The spray plant allowed the use of two pack acrylics and synthetic paints and could be heated to 60 degrees centigrade for quick drying. The painters involved in using the equipment undertook training in spray painting techniques.

Just one year later, the uncertain future of the ECW was again in the spotlight when, in July 1986, it was announced that Leyland Bus would be sold to a management team and the Lowestoft factory would not be part of the deal. While some may have expected this news, it still came as a shock and to many the thought that Lowestoft would lose such an important part of the industrial infrastructure and engineering skill base of the town was appalling. By the end of September 1986, the factory had finished all other work apart from the London Bus Olympian order. The following months saw the remaining vehicles of that order completed and leave for London. The demand for the Olympian bus continued for a number of years and with the ECW no longer in existence, the bodywork was built elsewhere.

The factory closed completely in January 1987 and after the sale of the site to a developer, all the buildings were demolished.

In addition to thousands of bodies built prior to the Second World War, during the post war years ECW had an impressive output with almost 27,000 bodies for use with chassis supplied by a variety of manufacturers. Some of the more noteworthy production runs were bodies for the following types of chassis or similar.

Bristol Lodekka	5218 bodies	Bristol VR series#	3494
Bristol K series#	3465	Bristol RE series#	2956
Bristol L series#	2155	Bristol MW	1913
Leyland Olympian#	1472	Bristol LS	1392
Bristol LH	1218		

Includes similar bodies used on other types of chassis

Eastern Coach Works was a major economic asset to Lowestoft and today no sign of the main factory exists, the site now being occupied by an assortment of warehouses, retail and trade outlets, a Post Office delivery office, car parks and roads. The only former ECW buildings in the town are those in Economy Road where a small satellite factory existed until 1957, and the remains of a weighbridge building and vacant site of the weighbridge in north Lowestoft. The site of the other weighbridge used by ECW was buried under a new road in 2006. The former buildings in Economy Road are to be demolished during 2007 as part of a regeneration plan and the site redeveloped.

Leyland Bus passed to Volvo in 1988 and included in their 2007 range of products is the Volvo Olympian, a very different vehicle to that seen at ECW. It seemed to many that after disposing of ECW, Leyland Bus could not survive!

SOME OTHER ASPECTS OF DAILY LIFE AT EASTERN COACH WORKS

Eastern Coach Works Sports & Social Club
Eastern Coach Works had very good sports and social facilities with tennis courts, a football pitch, cricket practice nets and a bowling green. The factory had a very active Sports & Social Club that at one time had up to 18 different sections and produced many excellent sportsmen and women who represented ECW and the town. Sports activities included football, cricket, angling, rifle shooting, snooker, archery, swimming and table tennis. There was a very popular horticultural section that organised two flower and vegetable shows each year and other club activities that included dancing, drama, pastimes and hobbies. Very competitive interdepartmental sports were played each year for the director's cups and trophies.

The spring of 1937 saw the launch of *The Hooter*, a club magazine that aimed to keep all employees and staff aware of the events in and around the factory, and contained results from the various sports sections, short stories, cooking items, fashion, cartoons and items of general interest. Many departments had their own social sections and organised outings, mystery tours and dinner dances/socials at Christmas. An annual feature of the Social Club was the Christmas Draw; this involved all parts of the factory with the actual draw being held just before Christmas in the canteen. At one time the Club owned an ECW bodied coach that was kept in superb condition and used for member's outings.

Mr. G. Harpour, who worked for many years in the Body Shop, was well known for his achievements whilst representing the ECW Pistol and Small Bore Rifle Club. He won many awards in national competitions. The ECW was considered to have one of the best industrial sports and social clubs in the country.

Unions

Unions played an important role at ECW in negotiating pay deals and bonus agreements, and generally protecting member's rights and interests. A number of trades were represented by their respective unions but the National Union of Vehicle Builders (NUVB) was the main union until 1972 when it amalgamated with the Transport and General Workers' Union.

The NUVB was established in 1919 by the amalgamation of the London and Provincial Coachmakers' Society, the Operative Coachmakers and Wheelwrights' Federal Labour Union, the London Coachsmiths and Vicemen's Trade Society and the United Kingdom Society of Coachmakers (founded in 1830). In 1925 it absorbed the Amalgamated Wheelwrights, Smiths and Kindred Trades Union and in 1948 the Wheelwrights and Coachmakers' Operative Union. In general, industrial disputes were rare at ECW, disagreements being usually settled with management before they got to the dispute stage. As well as the main union membership, the NUVB ran a Slate Club for those under 60 who paid into it each week. When a member was off work due to sickness, in addition to the statutory sick pay, they could get an additional payment from the Sick Fund. In the mid 1960s this was 20/- per week (£1) for the first eight weeks of sickness thereafter it dropped to 10/- (50p). A funeral allowance, raised by a levy of 1/- (5p) from each member, would be paid to a deceased member's next of kin. A levy could be raised whenever the officers considered it justified and any money left outstanding at the year end would be disposed by a "share out"; with the remaining money being divided up and returned to the members.

Holidays

In the early 1950s, the holiday entitlement at the factory was two weeks, this was always the last week in July and the first in August, during which time the factory closed. There were also six bank holidays. By the time ECW closed in 1987, the annual holiday entitlement had been extended to four weeks plus eight bank holidays.

Blood Donors

The National Blood Transfusion Service paid annual visits to the factory and many of the workforce gave blood. Two employees were awarded a gold badge for having given their 50th pint of blood. Sheet metal worker Christopher Howlett and materials controller Maurice Bird had been regular donors for many years.

War Memorials

With the closure of the factory the two War Memorials containing Rolls of Honour were transferred to the Lowestoft War Memorial Museum which is situated in the Sparrows Nest in Lowestoft. The Second World War memorial is a large metal plate with white lettering and the National Service memorial is a wooden plaque with gold lettering. There are the names of 30 employees on the World War Two memorial who lost their lives whilst serving in the Army, Royal Navy and Royal Air Force, and the names of two employees who were killed in 1952 are on the National Service memorial.

The well known front of the factory in Eastern Way seen during the last days before closure in 1987. For many years a scene of great activity, the presence of employees' cars parked in front of the doors signifies that much of the factory is empty with only three vehicles of the London Buses order to be seen, one of which is just visible through the glass in a door. Of the two 68 seat Olympians where the doors are open, the one on the left is L250 (D250FYM) and the other is L263(D263FUL). The last vehicle to leave the factory was L263 which was fitted with coach seats, while L250 had bus seats.
(Copyright Norman Fairhead)

Left - "We cover the country", an advertisement that needs no explanation.

Right - The quality and robustness of Lowestoft built bodywork is the main theme of this advertisement.
(Both copyright Past Times Prints)

Eastern Coach Works in the early 1960s

In 1963, a record of daily happenings and events at the Eastern Coach Works was made by a member of the workforce. The record is reproduced here as it was written, and therefore the reader must return to 1963 at a time when ECW was a leading manufacturer of bus and coach bodies in the British Isles.

The Year is 1963

The keystone to the practical side of the business is the Design Department. This is where the ideas are born and developed and where the stresses and strains to be encountered by the vehicle body are determined, the pleasing shapes and passenger comfort considered and the margins of material strength and public safety calculated. From the Design Department the determined data passes to the Drawing Office to be developed on paper to scale. The drawings then pass to the Setting Out Department for full size development. This is carried out by a team of development draughtsmen (Known as "Setters Out") on large plywood boards. From these full size boards, the various patterns are produced for the use of machine operators. This department also produces the jigs and formers required to obtain accuracy and uniformity in the various body shapes. Whilst this preliminary work is going on, a department attached to the Drawing Office is compiling schedules detailing the materials required for the production of the actual bodies. These schedules pass to the Purchasing Department, where the raw materials and numerous items of equipment are placed on order for delivery in time to meet production requirements.

Machined and processed parts pass from the production shops to the Finished Parts Stores, there to await requisition by the sub-assembly departments.

Modern mass production demands specialisation and in the interests of economy and output, the work of body erection is broken down into sub-assemblies. For this purpose the men work in "gangs", one "gang" building floors, another sides, another fronts, another roofs and so on, all of which are built on fixtures to ensure accuracy and to simplify the work of construction. The sub-assemblies then pass to the main assembly "gangs" for attachment to the chassis and the uniting of the sub-assemblies to form the completed body skeleton or framework. As soon as the framework is completed, the exterior panels of aluminium alloy are fitted before moving the vehicle. The body panelling is carried out in the body assembly shop. Much of the flat panelling is purchased to the exact sizes required, the only processing in this case being the punching of the fixing holes and the initial paint processing before fitting. There is of course a large amount of shaped panel work to be made and this is prepared beforehand in a modern shop equipped with both hand and power machinery. The pleasing dome shaped panels which streamline the front and rear of the body are "stretched" by forcing a die under hydraulic pressure into a sheet of soft aluminium. Much hand craft work in the way of forming, beating, welding, etc. is however necessary to obtain the tremendous variety of shapes required.

After panelling, the body mouldings are applied, these being fitted vertically and horizontally to seal the panel joints against the weather. The mouldings are screwed into position, the screw head recesses being pellet sealed to provide a flush finish and to seal the screw heads from the effects of moisture.

The body is now ready to move into the Paint Shop to be "cleaned off" and to receive its initial priming coat of paint. Also at this stage the work of finishing the interior of the body commences. Electric cables for lighting, signal bell and door operation, together with the numerous other items of electrical equipment are run through the body. Linoleum is applied to the floor by trimmers. The casing or side panels are covered in fabric (usually leathercloth) and interior ceiling panels are fitted. Floor treads are fixed where heavy wear takes place and the general interior furnishings are applied by the finishers. This work proceeds in conjunction with the painting process, daily the vehicle moves up the shop as it receives its various coats of paint, towards the Varnish Room.

Following the priming coat, each body receives four coats of paint viz: a sealing coat, an undercoat of the final colour required, followed by two coats of enamel. The vehicle then moves into the Varnish Room, which is heated, to receive its final two coats of clear varnish. This gives the body its lusterous finish and forms a protection film to the undercoats of colour.

During the varnishing process the room is closed to all workers except those engaged in the varnishing process. This precaution is necessary in order to ensure as far as possible a dustless atmosphere within the Varnish Room.

Following the varnish coats the vehicle moves forward into the Finishing Shop where the remaining fittings are applied. These include the body windows, seats, handrails, interior lamps, destination indicator fittings, etc.

On completion, and after fitters have checked the engine and tyres, the vehicle is road tested and weighed at one of two sites away from the factory. Any faults discovered during the road test are rectified before submitting the vehicle to the Ministry of Transport for Certification of Fitness for Public Service Operation. After this paintwork would be touched up and a thorough clean of the vehicle carried out before it finally leaves the factory for delivery to the operator.

A team of Inspectors check all materials for accuracy and quality and a routine inspection system operates at every stage of machining, body construction and finishing.

With the exception of tubular seat frames, all seats are manufactured on the premises by our own staff of skilled seat makers, sewing machinists and coach trimmers. A variety of materials are in current use for application, such as moquettes, hide and P.V.C. coated leathercloths. All seat cushions are of foam rubber, these being found most suitable both for passenger comfort and long service life. Handrails are of stainless steel, again formed to the required shape on the premises. Toughened safety glass bedded in rubber is employed throughout with the exception of the driver's windscreen; this is of laminated safety glass in case of breakage and the consequent possibility of obscuring the driver's vision through the shattering which can occur with toughened glass.

As it would be totally uneconomical to manufacture all the numerous fittings and component parts required, many proprietary articles are purchased from firms specialising in such items as seat frames, electrical fittings and lamps, roof ventilators, heating equipment, destination indicator gear, etc. These are "bought out" and only require to be fitted into position on the body when received.

The comparatively new material known as Fibre Glass Laminate is coming more prominently into use in omnibus body construction. At the moment however, its use is limited on Tilling vehicles to engine and bonnet cowling on double deck vehicles, interior parcel racks on certain models, rear corner panels on all models and certain small interior items. Further applications will no doubt be made if and where it appears to offer a definite advantage over alternative materials. All Public Service Vehicles must conform to specified standards of measurement, weight, stability, safety and comfort. The final operation required for each vehicle is certification by a Certifying Officer of the Ministry of Transport.

No vehicle can obtain a Road Licence without a Certificate of Fitness.

Some Body Types in Current Production

Road Passenger transport is becoming an increasingly competitive business as more people provide their own means of transport and the railways compete with comfortable and swift diesel and electric train services. In many instances, particularly in rural districts, the omnibus services operate at a heavy loss. Nevertheless, operators are under an obligation to provide public transport and one way of economising is to operate vehicles designed for the particular service for which they are required. To meet these demands, Eastern Coach Works produce a wide range of bodies from 26 seat capacity to 70 seat.

In the small capacity range, provision is made for one-man operation when the fares are collected by the driver when the passengers board the vehicle, the conductor being no longer required. This type of vehicle is in steady demand for rural service operation.

The SC

The popular type is a 35 seater body fitted to a Bristol chassis, powered by a Gardner 4 LK type forward engine and known as the SC lightweight vehicle. Fitted with electrically operated Glider type entrance doors, this vehicle serves the country district operator admirably. The initial cost is comparatively low and operation and maintenance costs are reduced to a minimum. Vehicle dimensions are 27ft. 6ins. long x 7ft 6ins wide and laden height 9ft 4ins. The unladen vehicle weight is 4 tons 2½ cwts.

The MW

Next in the range of single deck stage carriage bodies comes the 45 seater Medium Weight type which again can be adapted to one-man operation if required. Fitted to a Bristol under-floor engine chassis, this vehicle is the one most in demand for single deck service work. It can be powered by a 5 or 6 cylinder Gardner or a Bristol 6 cylinder engine to suit the type of territory to be covered. Dimensions are 30ft. long x 8 ft. wide and the laden height 10ft. 2ins. Unladen vehicle weight is 6 tons, 11½ cwts. Standard equipment includes heaters, demisters electrically operated entrance doors and parcel accommodation. Side sliding or hopper type ventilating windows are also fitted as standard. Safety Glass is fitted throughout as in the case of all ECW bodies.

The LD

In the double deck range, production is mainly concentrated on the Lodekka body, the output of which exceeds all other models. This vehicle possesses all the virtues of a highbridge body whilst maintaining a low overall height. The standard LD type is fitted with seats for 60 passengers, 27 in the lower saloon and 33 in the upper saloon. Manually operated doors can be fitted to enclose the rear platform if required. Dimensions for this model are 27ft. long x 8ft. wide, laden height 13ft. 3ins. and unladen weight 7 tons 14 cwts.

This vehicle supersedes both the highbridge and lowbridge models by combining all the desirable body features of both types and is in popular demand. The LD model is however, shortly due to be superseded by an improved version incorporating a flat floor in the lower saloon, thereby dispensing with the central sunk gangway in use on the LD model and providing easier access to the seats together with increased headroom above the seats.

The Lodekka vehicle is a joint product of Bristol Commercial Vehicles Limited and Eastern Coach Works Limited, the aluminium alloy body being built integrally with the chassis. A 70-seater 30 ft. long version of the Lodekka is also available to operators requiring this type of vehicle. All Lodekka models are fitted with forward engines which may be 5 or 6 cylinder Gardner, or 6 cylinder Bristol.

At the time of going to press (1963), there are some 2,300 Lodekka vehicles in operation throughout Great Britain from the highlands of Scotland to the Isle of Wight, and reports indicate that it is the most successful double deck passenger vehicle on the road to-day.

Limited Stop Service and Coach Vehicles

In the more luxurious class, two types of bodies are produced, the Express Carriage or limited stop service type and the Touring Coach type. The Express Carriage body is in fact a more luxurious version of the Stage Carriage body. Fitted with 41 or 43 coach type seats, this vehicle is designed for longer distance travel with limited stops, as distinct from stage to stage collection and discharge service. Certain refinements are added to enhance internal and external appearances and to provide additional passenger comfort.

Polished alloy mouldings are fitted to the exterior sides, front and rear. An attractive winged motif is fitted to the body front and seats are of the reclining type. Additional interior lighting provides more comfortable night travel and heater units are fitted as standard. Other standard items of equipment include electrically operated entrance doors, windscreen demisters, luggage accommodation,

sliding or hopper type ventilating windows, large roof ventilators, etc. This vehicle provides a medium between the more utility type of stage carriage body and the touring coach type, and is in popular demand. Fitted to the Bristol Medium Weight chassis with underfloor engine of the 5 or 6 cylinder Gardner or 6 cylinder Bristol type, this vehicle is in wide use on long distance service work and is adaptable to either summer or winter use.

The MW Touring Coach

The Touring Coach body is of course the last word in luxury travel and the early part of each year sees ECW busily concentrating on this type of body in order to deliver in time for early summer use by operators. In the annual Coach Rallies held at Clacton-on-Sea, Brighton and London, Bristol/ECW coaches have been successful in winning the following awards:-

1955
Clacton-on-Sea

Winner of the "Lister Cup"
Operator - Eastern Counties Omnibus Co. Limited.

1956
Brighton

Winner of the Premier Award "The Brighton Trophy"
Winner of the "Lister Cup" (second time)
Winner of the "Autobrite Cup"
Operator - Eastern Counties Omnibus Company Limited.

1957
Battersea Park, London

Winner of the "Lister Cup" (third time).
Operator - Eastern National Omnibus Co. Ltd.

1958
Brighton

Winner of the "Premier" Award in the Concours d' Elegance
Winner of the "'Clacton Trophy"
Operator - Thames Valley Traction Co. Ltd.

This outstanding record of success speaks well for the quality and design of the Bristol/ECW Coach. Whilst quietly pleasing in appearance, the emphasis has always been on maximum passenger comfort rather than on a lavishly garnished exterior and these desirable features undoubtedly appealed to the competition judges.

Again, a choice of engines of the 5 or 6 cylinder Gardner, or the 6 cylinder Bristol is available. Body dimensions are 30ft. long x 8ft. wide, and up to 36ft. long x 8ft. 2ins. wide.

A wide choice of equipment is available to suit the requirements of coach operators. This includes large Perspex glazed roof ventilators, hopper type ventilating windows, heaters, adjustable reclining seats, glazed roof eaves, public address equipment, sun blinds, luggage accommodation and many other refinements. A toughened glass screen isolates the driver from the saloon without obscuring the passengers' forward vision. Large front and side windows provide a panoramic view in every direction. A glazed front roof canopy is also available if required.

These coaches are designed for tourist travel and provide the highest possible degree of clear vision and luxury comfort under all conditions. Seating capacities range from 30 to 41 passengers.

The SC Lightweight Coach

A coach version of the SC vehicle mentioned earlier is manufactured and a number of these are in operation by Tilling Companies. They are particularly adaptable to short pleasure trips such as half-day excursion runs in coastal areas, evening trips to the countryside and local theatre party journeys throughout the year. With normal seating accommodation for 33 passengers the SC coach is an economical proposition for the type of work described. Easily manoeuvrable for country district operation there is also a limited demand for the SC coach by rural operators. The body is mounted on a Bristol chassis and fitted with a forward engine of the Gardner 4 LD type, the same chassis in fact as that in use with the stage carriage body version. Certain minor refinements are, however, incorporated in the interior and exterior of the body to enhance appearance and to provide additional travel comforts. The front bulkhead is cut away above waist level to allow full forward vision by passengers. Heaters and demisters are fitted as standard and a polished alloy grille in modern styling enhances the exterior frontal appearance. A manually operated sliding type entrance door is employed. This vehicle is undoubtedly an ideal type for short journey pleasure travel.

Modern development and the now almost continuous flow of new materials becoming available, call for constant research and experiment into new fields of body design. Types in current production may now be quite obsolete in a short space of time. With the ever increasing competition from other forms of transport, Public Service Operators must be provided with vehicles incorporating the most up to date improvements in order to attract additional traffic.

This is constantly borne in mind by the ECW management and staff and no effort is spared in aiming to keep to the forefront of development by constant liaison with operators and by experimental and trial application within our Works.

Service Life of the Modern Vehicle

The age old craft of coach building has changed radically since the days of the stage coach and hansom cab. The handcraft has largely disappeared. Timber and iron in the framework have been superseded by light alloys. The polished wood formerly used for interior decoration has been replaced by polished aluminium and plastic materials. These new materials combined with improved roads and improved chassis suspension systems have all contributed to provide a longer period of service life for the road vehicle.

Immediately before the 1939-45 war, ECW bodies were built mainly from teak, this being the best rot-resisting timber commercially available at that time. Bodies were then planned for a ten year life although this was seldom attained. The inevitable attack by moisture would invariably rot the more vulnerable parts of the framework well within this planned period. Not so with the modern alloy body, one can confidently expect a service life of 15-20 years with proper maintenance and attention. Even where timber is used in the framework the danger of rot from moisture has largely disappeared with the introduction of modern glazing methods and sealing materials.

Bodies now produced are accurately built to within fine limits thus enabling a parts replacement service to be maintained and a consequent speedy return to service of vehicles following overhaul or accident repair by operators.

Every component part on all models of ECW bodies bears a part number and by quoting the part number or numbers required, the customer is assured of quick delivery of accurate replacements. This has been made possible only by the standardisation of the various body "shells" and the introduction of precision methods in manufacture.

Materials employed in Manufacture

High grade materials play an all important part in the manufacture of ECW bodies. Generally speaking, all raw materials and proprietary fittings used are the best of their respective kinds. The theory that the best is the cheapest in the long run is proved by the service life obtained from vehicles in operation, many of which serve industrial areas and are subjected to the most severe conditions of wear and tear. A few typical examples of materials in standard use are as follows:-

Body Structure
Aluminium, Manganese-Magnesium Alloy extrusions specially treated for strength and ductility.

Panelling
Aluminium, Manganese - Magnesium alloy sheet in various hardness and gauges.

Handrails, Grab Rails, etc.
Stainless Steel.

Glass
Toughened safety glass, Laminated safety glass.

Floorboards (Where Used)
First quality Douglas Fir.

Structural Timber (Where Used)
English Oak, Siamese Yang, Mahogany.

Floor Coverings
High quality non-slip linoleum.

Glazing Medium
High quality patented section weatherproof rubber.

Seat Frames
Tubular steel with polished stainless steel top rails.

Seat Cushions
High quality foam rubber.

Seat Upholstery
First quality moquettee and hide.

Body Trimming
High quality Leathercloth or PVC fabric.

Platform and Staircase Treads (Double Deck Bodies)
Non slip wire woven fabric in Aluminium Alloy channel base.

Interior and Exterior Paintwork
High quality undercoats, enamels and varnishes, brush applied.

These represent but a few of the many items of raw materials employed, the same attention to high grade however applies throughout, even to the bolts, nuts, screws and rivets which to us are equally important where quality is concerned.

Miscellaneous Body Types Produced by E.C.W.

Whilst ECW are mainly engaged in the production of PSV bodies, facilities exist for the manufacture of bodies of other types to customers special requirements.

Recent departure from PSV bodies has been the manufacture of two 56 seat railbus bodies for British Railways. Fitted to Bristol under-carriages, these railbuses are in operation in Scotland.

Lorry cabs, Flats, Vans and Pantechnicons have also been produced.

A further recent diversion has been the manufacture of a mobile laboratory body for British Railways. Mounted on a Bedford 4-wheel drive RLH chassis, a type used extensively by the British Army, this vehicle is equipped with a heat insulated body. In the front portion is a photographic dark room complete with water tanks, stainless steel sink, heaters and extraction fan. A larger section is fitted out for the reception of electronic equipment for the testing of bridges and other structures. The body is also fitted with heaters.
The interior walls throughout are lined with light pastel "Formica". A ladder attached to the rear of the body gives access to a roof gangway.

It will be seen therefore, that as long as the requirement is a vehicle body, ECW possess the facilities and the "know how" to build it. This is only as it should be. After 48 years in the road vehicle business a tremendous amount of information, knowledge and experience is necessarily gained.

No precise information is available regarding the body output of the early days, but the total number placed on the roads from available records runs into many thousands of bodies of all types.

Labour Force

Of the total labour force of 1,075, over 800 are production workers, the remainder comprising office and administrative staff, storekeepers, labourers, etc. The production workers are made up of craftsmen of various trades roughly as follows:-

Woodcutting, Setters Out, Metal Cutting Machinists	56
Bodybuilders	200
Body Finishers	114
Coach Trimmers	66
Seatmakers	13
Painters	110
Panel beaters and Sheet Metal Workers	128
Engineering Fitters	95
Electricians	23

Many of these tradesmen are people with long terms of service with the Company and in some cases their fathers and sons worked at ECW as well.

Travelling about the country, particularly at holiday times, these folk must experience a thrill of pride at seeing, and no doubt often using, the vehicles they have helped to build and which they have no difficulty in identifying.

Customers

Here is a list of some Tilling undertakings operating ECW bodied Public Service Vehicles:-

Alexander, A., Falkirk. Scotland
Brighton Hove & District Omnibus Co. Ltd., Brighton
Bristol Omnibus Co. Ltd., Bristol
Central S.M.T. Co. Ltd., Motherwell, Scotland
Crosville Motor Services Ltd., Chester.
Cumberland Motor Services, Ltd., Cumberland

Durham District Omnibus Co. Ltd.
Eastern Counties Omnibus Co. Ltd., Norwich
Eastern National Omnibus Co. Ltd., Chelmsford
Hants & Dorset Motor Services Ltd., Bournemouth
Lincolnshire Road Car Co. Ltd., Lincoln
Mansfield & District Traction Co. Ltd., Mansfield
Midland General Omnibus Co, Ltd., Nottingham
Red & White Services Ltd., Chepstow, Monmouthshire
Scottish Omnibuses Ltd., Edinburgh, Scotland
Sheffield Joint Omnibus Committee
Southern National Omnibus Co. Ltd., Exeter
South Midland Motor Services Ltd., Reading
Southern Vectis Omnibus Co. Ltd., Isle of Wight
Thames Valley Traction Co. Ltd., Reading
Tilling Transport (B.T.C.) Ltd., London
United Automobile Services Ltd., Darlington
United Counties Omnibus Co. Ltd., Northampton
United Welsh Services Ltd., Swansea
Western National Omnibus Co. Ltd., Exeter
Western S.M.T. Co. Ltd., Kilmarnock, Scotland
West Yorkshire Road Car Co. Ltd., Harrogate
Wilts & Dorset Motor Services Ltd., Salisbury

In addition to the above, ECW bodies have been supplied to many municipal undertakings and other Public Transport Authorities.

These include:-

Great Yarmouth Borough Transport
London Transport
Lowestoft Corporation Transport
Middlesbrough Corporation
Rochdale Corporation

What of the Future?

As we have already observed, the demand for Public Transport has tended to decline during recent years. It is, however, by no means certain that this trend will continue. There is an increasing tendency to build housing estates on the outskirts of towns for two reasons. Firstly, because town centres are already largely built up, and secondly because people prefer to live in these fringe areas rather than in the town centres. This must lead to increased application for public transport to be provided to such districts. Furthermore, the probable dispersal of industry in the future must also call for more public transport services.

Regarding coach travel, the tourist trade is undoubtedly on the increase. Each year sees more of our people taking continental holidays by coach and more people from abroad are visiting and touring Britain. The outlook for the trade is therefore by no means gloomy.

The future outlook naturally concerns the vehicle builder just as much as the operator, in as much as the livelihood of both is dependent on the patronage of the travelling public.

Eastern Coach Works is kept constantly in touch with these future probabilities and advance plans are made accordingly.

New types placed in production to-day were no doubt planned, prototype built and tested two years or more ago. Research and experimental work goes on continuously in order to keep to the forefront of development. In such a highly competitive industry no one can afford to lag behind in this respect.

1962 saw the completion of 50 years of steady progress of our Company and we have every reason to look to the future with confidence.

Footnote - 2007

As has been already mentioned, whilst under Leyland control, Eastern Coach Works closed permanently in January 1987. The quality of workmanship, commitment and range of skills shown by those employed at Eastern Coach Works was truly exceptional. The major loss to Lowestoft of this high profile and much respected vehicle body manufacturer has never been made good.

Fortunately, a great many vehicles with bodies built at Eastern Coach Works survive, the great majority of these are preserved, but some remain in daily service mainly on contract, special or charter work. Most of these tend to be Leyland Olympians with body work produced in the final years of ECW and a few Bristol VRTs, some of which are used on seasonal work where they are used "topless" at popular seaside towns such as Scarborough and Whitby.

A member of the Lodekka family, Lincolnshire 2514 (VFE963) was completed around the time that this article was written. It had body 13821 configured as H33/27RD and chassis FS5G 214.169. No. 2514 is seen here at Scunthorpe on 21st May 1980.
(Copyright Malcolm White/Alan Robinson)

Working at Eastern Coach Works

Norman Fairhead
Body Shop 1955-86

On leaving school at the age of 15, I had an interview at the Eastern Coach Works with the Manager, Mr. Alf Tattersall. The interview had been arranged by Mr. George White, the Labour Officer at the factory. It was often the case that a son would follow his father at the factory, and indeed both my father and grandfather worked there. I was offered a five year apprenticeship in the Body Shop at a take home wage of £1-18s- 0d. for a 44 hour week, and initially worked in the Jig Shop on the construction of side sections, before moving on to floors. The bodies we were building were for the last traditional "highbridge" buses built at the factory.

The foreman, Mr. Les Saunders, later moved me on to assembly work on the Lodekka LD double deck bodies that were constructed of wood and aluminium.

A scene during the early years of Norman's career at ECW. West Yorkshire DX15 (OWX159), a Bristol LD6B with H33/27RD body, was completed in October 1955. *(Copyright Phil Burcham)*

I was put with two assemblers, Mr. Ted Ellis and Mr. Wilf Bush, forming the usual gang of three. At times when we needed extra help Mr. Alec Wilson joined us.

We would be allocated a Lodekka chassis and would then go to the stores and withdraw all the materials needed for the job. After preparing the chassis, which would include positioning and fixing the bulkhead and the aluminium floor section, we would request the side sections that would be brought from the Jig Shop manually on a barrow. We would position and align these, and then bolt them to the chassis.

My job was to prepare the intermediate roof sticks and fix them in place, while the other gang members would be working on either the front or the rear. We would work together laying the intermediate floor, which was made of tongue and groove floorboards. On completion we would be ready for the roof section. This was carried through on a barrow and then lifted manually into place and involved Body Shop members on the ground, lifting the roof on props to those on the top deck. The roof was then fixed in place. Other sections that were lifted into place were for the front and back of the vehicle. The stairs were constructed in position. When the body was completed it was inspected and passed for painting, panelling and moulding. The body stayed in the same position for all of this work to be carried out, which also included all the electrical wiring.

On the introduction of the Olympian contract, an overhead lifting system was installed in the factory and a line system introduced. I was placed on stage one of the assembly operation, which involved two people. Unlike the previous system, the intermediate roof was jig built and supplied complete. After positioning the side sections the fixing involved aligning predrilled holes and fastening with Audelok type fixings, this operation was completed in 1½ days before the vehicle was moved on to the next stage of production. Then the same operation would be repeated on the next vehicle.

When an Olympian was moved to the paint shop, the exterior would be cleaned and masked, and the floor covering would be laid before going in the spray booth. This was enclosed, with only those involved in the work allowed access. On completion of spraying, the interior furnishings and fittings would be put in place.

The scene inside the Body Shop in the 1950s with work mainly concentrated on Bristol Lodekka and
Bristol LS vehicles with Norman in the white shirt working at the bench between the two Lodekka chassis.
(Norman Fairhead Collection)

Following this, the glazing was fitted, the seats installed and finally the vehicle would be made ready for a road test.

If no faults had been found during the road test, the paint would be touched up and a complete clean of the vehicle carried out. The bus was then ready for delivery to the owner.

Traditionally, vehicle bodies had been hand painted at the ECW, with a number of coats of paint and varnish applied whilst the vehicle was in an enclosed heated bay. Also, chassis were at one time individually driven from Bristol to Lowestoft. The driver had little protection from the weather and sometimes had to be helped off the chassis on arrival. Later the chassis were transported to Lowestoft by lorry.

The day to day routine at the ECW was often interspersed with bouts of harmless fun. On one occasion in the Body Shop, a vehicle in for attention had seats in place, and those staying for lunch sat in it. One person fell asleep in the bus and the others, after finishing their lunch, crept off and returned to work leaving him asleep. Their sleeping workmate eventually awoke 10 minutes into work time and was met by the others banging on metal plates with hammers to welcome him back.

Dances were held monthly in the works canteen with the Hawaiian Beats, a popular local group and other groups playing for all types of dancing. An annual Christmas party was also held in the canteen with entertainment and a tea being laid on for the children.

Mr. David Bullard
Trimmers Shop 1953-87

I left school in December 1952 at the age of 15 and careers advice in those days was very sparse, but during the last year at school we were taken around various local firms to give us an idea as to what employment was available. While visiting the annual Lowestoft Homes and Trades Exhibition held at the Palais de Dance I saw a trimmer at work on a stand and thought that is what I would like to do. I applied for a job at ECW and had an interview with the labour officer Mr. George White. Following the interview, I received an offer of a job in the Trimming Shop and started on 3rd January 1953 at 0730hrs at the Economy Works in South Lowestoft, which was a satellite to the main Eastern Way factory. My pay was 9¾d. per hour for a 44 hour week, some days we worked 0730hrs -1730hrs and others 0730-1700hrs with an hour for lunch. My apprenticeship included attending a course on Commercial Motor Body Work at night school for two hours on two evenings each week. The shop in Economy Works was quite large and divided into various operations namely squabs (seat back rests) cushions, cutting out and sewing machinists. Also on site were the seatmakers who made the wooden frame work for the seats before they were trimmed. The foreman of the Trimming Shop was Mr. Jack Baldwin to whom I reported. The chargehands were Mr. Fred Howlett - in charge of cutting out and sewing machinists, Mr. Percy Chapman - leading hand in charge of cushions, Mr. Len Davey - leading hand in charge of the squab section and Mr. Harry Green responsible for inspection. With the apprenticeship starting when we were 16, for the first year I was cutting out pieces of material such as leather, rexine, calico, hessian and foam rubber and stacking cushions and finished squabs. We also had to do the morning and afternoon tea round and take orders for rolls, dinners and cakes from the canteen for which we were paid a small commission, and answer the telephone in the foreman's office if he was not there. After a while I was introduced to trimming, and the first seats I worked on were driver's seats of which I was expected to do 15 each week.

After a while I progressed to working on standard squabs and coach seats. Sometimes during the early part of your apprenticeship you had to do close trimming and linoleum laying, this was carried out at the main factory in Eastern Way. Close trimming involved sticking rexine to interior panels of the vehicles and to many mouldings. Linoleum laying meant covering the floors by cutting and sticking linoleum down, in the early days this was real linoleum, but as the years passed "Treadmaster", a mixture of cork and rubber, was introduced. Stairs on double deck vehicles were covered with nosings fixed on the leading edge. The floors and entrances of coaches were carpeted and the back of the well covered in matching vinyl sheet, again with nosings on the leading edges of the stairs. One operation that was awkward was close trimming the interior rear dome in coaches for which you were given a piece of rexine. By stretching, pushing and pulling this had to be stuck on without creases, folds or marks. In charge of lino and close trimming was Mr. Ted Reynolds.

The method of fixing the covers on seats, squabs and cushions was by tacking or gimp pins. Headrests on some coaches were moulded on a solid block of wood. After soaking the leather in warm water, it was stretched onto the mould and left to dry, then it was marked out and the ends stitched on. They were then ready to be put on the ply back board over a moulded latex cushioning. The edges of coach seats were finished off with piping and beading, and the back of the squab finished off with rexine in my early days. There was so much vandalism on buses that eventually a hard surface plastic laminate called "Wareite" was used on the interior panels and screens of buses.

Most seats on coaches or standard bodies consisted of a combination of leather and vinyl facings and ends, and moquette panels but sometimes vinyl or leather was used for the entire seat. Fluted squabs and cushions were also produced in vinyl or leather for some operators, this consisted of a piece of leather/vinyl and a piece of calico stitched together and the flutes, about 1¾ ins. wide, stuffed with wadding.

Hand stitching was used very little, usually only on the odd occasion when a neat finish on the back of a seat was required and tacks, gimp pins or staples would look out of place.

Big changes took place in the early to mid 1970s when pneumatic staple guns and spray guns were introduced, and air tools became the norm throughout the factory although low voltage electric drills were used right up to the last day.

Examples of the skill of the seat maker, machinists and trimmer

Left - The upper deck of a Olympian coach
(Copyright J. & F. Shipley)
Above - The interior of a Bristol LS coach.
(ECW)

The Final Years
Building the Olympians

An order for 35 Olympian buses from Lothian Regional Transport appeared in the 1982 build programme and this was followed by other orders from the same operator. By 1986, a total of 127 ECW Olympians had been supplied to Lothian with many of the earlier vehicles having Bristol produced chassis. Displaying trade plates, Lothian 694 is seen here in Eastern Way about to leave the factory in December 1982 on a road test with an inspector on board. Two other Lothian Olympians are parked on the apron behind 694 and all three have missing front grills. This particular vehicle with body 25198 and chassis ONTL11/2R ON509 was later registered OFS694Y and as with all 35 in the batch, was configured H50/31D giving 81 seat capacity. The Lothian Olympians were just over 33ft. in length and remained in service with that operator until 2003. The superb ease of access to the factory from Eastern Way is well demonstrated in this and other photographs found in this book and for the enthusiast, the ECW premises were one of the easiest in UK to view PSVs during construction.

(Copyright Robert Ranger)

At the time when most production at ECW was focussed on the London Buses order, two further chassis are seen here arriving from Workington.
(Copyright Norman Fairhead)

Preparing to unload the two chassis. *(Copyright Norman Fairhead)*

A single chassis arrives at ECW from Workington.
(Copyright Norman Fairhead)

Preparing to unload the chassis.
(Copyright Norman Fairhead)

The full chassis park and on the left, one of the ten coaches with ECW bodywork completed in 1986 for San Francisco operator Gray Line. This particular vehicle is Gray Line 610 (2W98573) and carries body 26361. In the distance can be seen the rather neglected privately owned Bristol FLF6B mentioned elsewhere in this book. Those chassis that can be identified are part of the London Buses order.
(Copyright Norman Fairhead)

Another view of the park full of Olympian chassis. As in the previous photograph, all those that can be identified are destined to join London Buses fleet once their bodywork is complete. Many tend to forget that the Olympian was originally a Bristol design.
(Copyright Norman Fairhead)

Body Shop - Olympian chassis
floor preparation.
(*Copyright Norman Fairhead*)

Body Shop - Olympian with floor
section complete.
(*Copyright Norman Fairhead*)

Body Shop - Prepared chassis at Stage One ready for assembly of body sections.
(*Copyright Norman Fairhead*)

Body Shop - Leyland chassis ONTL11/2RSp ON2022 on which body 26247 would be assembled, on display at the Open Day on 20th July 1985. When completed, this vehicle became Maidstone & District 5450 (C450BKM), configured as CH45/28F. In this view the chassis has one side section, the intermediate roof and staircase in position.
(*Copyright Norman Fairhead*)

Body Shop - Chassis preparation with construction of an intermediate roof in the foreground.
(*Copyright Norman Fairhead*)

Body Shop - Stage One with chassis awaiting offside side section. (*Copyright Norman Fairhead*)

Body Shop - Stage One assembly with Norman Fairhead on the left and Ernie Button on the right. Norman and Ernie are working on a chassis that will eventually form part of London Buses L179.
(Copyright Norman Fairhead)

Body Shop - A demonstration during the 1985 Open Day by Foreman Ray Durrant who is positioning a near side section.
(Copyright Norman Fairhead)

Body Shop - Chassis with side
section in place.
(Copyright Norman Fairhead)

Body Shop - Chassis with
temporary engine supports in place
and intermediate roof in position.
David Thorpe is on the left and
Ernie Button on the right.
(Copyright Norman Fairhead)

Olympians all destined to join the London Buses fleet under construction at the rear of the Body Shop.
(All Copyright Norman Fairhead)

Body Shop - Stage One construction, fixing Olympian front section. (*Copyright Norman Fairhead*)

Body Shop - General view of Olympians at Stage One and showing Demag overhead hoist system. (*Copyright Norman Fairhead*)

Body Shop - Olympian with Stage
Two construction completed.
(Copyright Norman Fairhead)

Body Shop - A completed staircase
for an Olympian.
(Copyright Norman Fairhead)

Body Shop - Painting the underneath of an Olympian staircase.
(*Copyright Norman Fairhead*)

Body Shop - Arthur Smith positioning a Olympian staircase on a chassis. (*Copyright Norman Fairhead*)

Body Shop - View of a Roof Jig with the Body Shop office on the left. (*Copyright Norman Fairhead*)

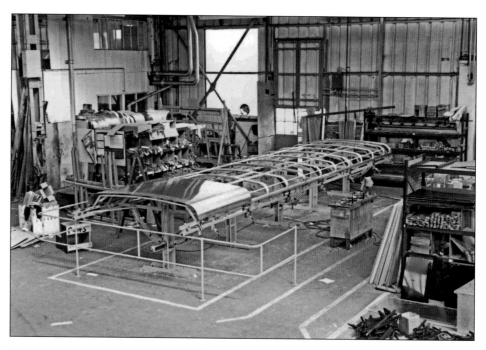

Body Shop - Gary Peck in the Jig Shop working on intermediate roof construction.
(*Copyright Norman Fairhead*)

Body Shop - Jig Shop with Terry
Rawston in the centre.
(*Copyright Norman Fairhead*)

Body Shop - Roof Jig construction
with David Sword on the left, and
Kenny Smith working on a roof.
(*Copyright Norman Fairhead*)

Body Shop - Olympians at Stages Two and Three of construction. (*All Copyright Norman Fairhead*)

Body Shop - Olympians at Stages Three and Four with panelling and moulding in progress. A rear dome can be seen lying on the floor on the right. (*Copyright Norman Fairhead*)

Body Shop - An Olympian at Stage Four in a moulding bay.
(*Copyright Norman Fairhead*)

Paint Shop - Preparing a body for painting. (*Copyright Norman Fairhead*)

Paint Shop - Body cleaned and masked. (*Copyright Norman Fairhead*)

An unpainted London Buses Olympian.
(*Copyright Norman Fairhead*)

Painted and unpainted London Buses Olympians in the Paint Shop. (*Copyright Norman Fairhead*)

Spray Booth - Rear view of a London Buses
Olympian bus ready for spray painting
(*Copyright Norman Fairhead*)

Spray Booth - Front view of a painted
Olympian bus.
(*Copyright Norman Fairhead*)

Spray Booth - Front view of a London Buses
Olympian after spray painting.
(Copyright Norman Fairhead)

Spray Booth - Rear view of a London Buses
Olympian after spray painting.
(Copyright Norman Fairhead)

Paint shop - A partly glazed
Olympian.
(*Copyright Norman Fairhead*)

Finishing/Paint Shop - Painting has
been completed and the
Olympian is now ready for
interior finishing.
(*Copyright Norman Fairhead*)

Paint Shop - Interior finishing at
the front of the shop.
(*Copyright Norman Fairhead*)

Finishing Shop - An Olympian with
glazing complete and seats fitted.
(*Copyright Norman Fairhead*)

Testing for water leaks on London Buses
L131 (D131FYM). Chassis ONLXB/1RH
ON2413 and body 26449 were used for
this bus. *(Copyright Norman Fairhead)*

EX56 was built as a demonstrator for sending to Thailand
and is seen here being inspected using the Hywena lifts
on 2nd September 1985. Amongst other special features,
EX56 was fitted with windows suitable for the Thailand
climate. This bus was originally intended to be Lothian
770 (B770GSC), with body 26001.
(Copyright Norman Fairhead)

Another view of London Buses L131 undergoing a water test whilst being checked for leaks. *(Copyright Norman Fairhead)*

The demonstrator for Thailand on the Hywema lifts on 2nd September 1985 from a different angle. *(Copyright Norman Fairhead)*

Finishing Shop - A bus ready for final work
to be carried out.
(Copyright Norman Fairhead)

Finishing Shop - Three London buses await
final stage finishing and touch up.
(Copyright Norman Fairhead)

The Hywema lifts in use again this time on Reading Transport 84 (D84UTF). This coach comprised chassis ONLXCT/IRH ON10206 and body 26456 configured as CH39/27F. It was one of five supplied to Reading in 1986 which were intended for use on the Goldline express service between Reading and London.
(Both Copyright Norman Fairhead)

Completed London Buses L143 (D143FYM) and Reading Transport 83(D83UTF) are seen in the PDI Area in 1986 where pre-delivery checks were carried out. London L143 had chassis ONLXB/1RH ON2426 and H42/26D body 26468, while Reading 83 had chassis ONLXCT/1RH ON10202 and CH39/27F body 26455.
(*Copyright Norman Fairhead*)

London Buses L258 (D258FYM) with body 26595 and chassis ONLXB/IRH ON2640 represents the completed product and for us, the last view from inside a factory building that today is a car park and delivery area.
Olympian production was moved to other plants when Leyland decided that ECW was not required and closed the factory.
(*Copyright Norman Fairhead*)

A view from outside the factory in the last days before closure of two of the final vehicles to leave ECW. The very last bus completed at the factory was London Buses L263 (D263FUL) which is on the right. L263 comprised body 26600 and chassis ONLXB/1RH ON 2645.
(*Copyright Norman Fairhead*)

L263 is recorded here on the last day at the front of the factory, which was later destined to be demolished. Immediately behind the Olympian is the Electricians Shop.
The closure resulted in another example of a centre of engineering excellence disappearing in Lowestoft and it set a trend for future years in the town.
(*Copyright Norman Fairhead*)

In the 1980s, large numbers of Olympians with bodywork by Eastern Coach Works could be found at work at the same time in two capital cities. This fact underlined the quality of the work produced by the skilled tradesmen and women at ECW and brought much pride and satisfaction to the workforce. It is regrettable that at a time when quality products continued to be made at Lowestoft, Leyland was rolling out a programme of redundancies for the workforce with a view to closing the plant, in spite of the ongoing demand for the products made there. We have seen how 260 Olympians were constructed for London and this view of Lothian Regional Transport 683 (OFS683Y), albeit with a missing radiator grill, represents over 120 similar buses delivered between 1982 and 1986 that could be found at work in the Edinburgh area. No. 683 is seen here at the factory in November 1982 and had body 25187 configured as H50/31D, with chassis ONTL11/2R ON467. (*Copyright Robert Ranger*)

Around The Factory

Pay day amongst the Olympians. Foreman Two Albert Beckett utilises the pay desk to hand out pay packets between Stages One and Two in the Body Shop.
(Copyright Norman Fairhead)

Paint Section - Hand Painting area and Dipping Trough.
(Copyright Norman Fairhead)

General view of the Paint Shop
(Copyright Norman Fairhead)

Body shop office and the bolt and
screw store
(Copyright Norman Fairhead)

Two views of the Panel Shop
(Copyright Norman Fairhead)

The Saw Mill

Top - Wood Section
Bottom - Metal Section
(Both Copyright Norman Fairhead)

The Glass Fibre Shop
(Copyright Norman Fairhead)

The Fitters Shop
(Copyright Norman Fairhead)

The completion of the 1000th Lodekka at ECW was marked by having an official photograph taken with many of the workforce present. Usually on such occasions it is the management and board members that take priority in photographs, but on this occasion it is those that "produced the goods" that are seen here. The celebrity bus was destined for Essex based Eastern National. On the right is the 999th Lodekka bodied at ECW and completing the picture are a few others, some of which are destined for Scottish operators. *(ECW)*

Machinists at ECW in the late 1960s
Front Row - Pauline Dunnett, Lenny Davey (Foreman), Gillian Smith, Irene Saunders, Ann Smith
Back Row - Wendy Prime, Moran Newrick, Ethel Welch, Janet Shipley, Pamela Leach, Muriel Crowe, John Pearson (Chargehand)
(J. & F. Shipley Collection)

After working in the same factory for a great many years, when retirement comes the last hours of employment can become quite emotional. These scenes were recorded in the Glaziers Shop on the last day of service for two long serving ECW employees.
(Norman Fairhead Collection)

Top - A group of colleagues are assembled to wish Ernie Fairhead all the best for the future on his retirement in 1973. Ernie is standing in front of the "Well Done Ernie" banner. A vehicle windscreen is on the bench in front of him.

Bottom - A similar event was held for Bill Fletcher on his last day of service. Here Bill, on the right, is being presented with his retirement gift by Foreman Ernie Green.

Arthur Smith on the left, Foreman Two Albert Beckett in the centre and on the right David Thorpe, discuss an aspect of the bodywork on an Olympian chassis.
(Copyright Norman Fairhead)

It was usual for a collection to be made to buy a present for a colleague who was getting married and here Foreman Ray Durrant is presenting Mark Munnings with his wedding present in the Body Shop.
(Copyright Norman Fairhead)

Ray Godbold was the centre of attention in this presentation. He is seen here on the right holding the gift, surrounded by work colleagues.
(Copyright Norman Fairhead)

The date is 21ˢᵗ November 1986, and the workforce is being reduced in stages during the last months prior to closure. On Friday afternoons it was usual for a "get together" to be arranged for those leaving. In this scene, from left to right are Owen Rogers, Ray Turrell, Dick Doddington, Tony Kent, Ernie Button, Colin Hawes, Mark Munnings, Ivan Harvey, Keith Ellison and Brian Gooch.
(Copyright Norman Fairhead)

Another Friday afternoon during the last few weeks prior to closure and another "get together" as Leyland makes more employees redundant and moves work that should have been carried out at ECW, to other Leyland factories. (Copyright Norman Fairhead)

As closure approached, many group photographs were taken in the various shops. In the Trimmers Shop we find in the front row of this group from left to right are Phillip Proudfoot, David Pearson, David Slater, Gordon Boyce, David Bullard, Peter Muirhead (Foreman) and Colin Wilton. At the back are Ray Tripp, Frank Shipley, Ricky Palmer, Steve Capps, Gordon Brundle, Ian Slater and Robert Garlick. (Copyright J. & F. Shipley)

In a rapidly emptying factory, we find a group of Body Shop personnel. From left to right are Norman Fairhead, Foreman Ray Durrant, John Gardiner, Ernie Button, John Burgess, Foreman Two Albert Beckett, Dick Doddington, Arthur Smith, Malcolm Whaley, Ray Hubble, Vic Mortishire and Roy Cook.
(Copyright Norman Fairhead)

As the factory emptied, the job of clearing out got underway. Seen gathered around a skip are, from left to right, Keith Ellison, Norman Ferguson, Ernie Button, Ivan Harvey and David "Yogi" Mitchell.
(Copyright Norman Fairhead)

Vehicles at the factory - Visiting

Buses and coaches with bodywork produced at the factory returned there for a number of reasons including repairs, repainting and modifications

Southdown Motor Services 1246 (GUF746) was one of 25 similar coaches ordered in 1947 with Leyland Tiger PS1 chassis. It was fitted with body 1640 that could seat 31 passengers and had large full depth sliding windows.

The reason for the visit to ECW is not immediately clear although it could be to repair the scratches, dents and marks on the body or more likely, to replace the windows that, apparently, were found not too satisfactory in every day service.

In both these photographs, 1246 is seen at the front of the factory in Eastern Way. *(Both ECW)*

ECOC 251(PCL251W), a 1980 Bristol VRT made a return visit to ECW in August 1984 for the application of overall Radio Broadland advertising. This VRT was withdrawn from service in the spring of 1998 and is believed scrapped later that year. The H43/31F body carried by 251 was 24614 and the chassis was VRT/SL3/6LXB/2569. No. 251 carried other overall advertising during its life including that for Lathams and The Living Jungle.

Top - The final touching up has been completed.
Bottom - Completed and waiting to return to ECOC.
(Both Copyright Norman Fairhead)

Many preserved ECW bodied vehicles attended the Open Day on 20th July 1985. Completed in January 1964, this Bristol RELH6G comprises body13739 in C47F configuration on chassis 212.027. It was originally United Welsh 18 (375GWN), although it was renumbered during 1965 as 52, followed in 1970 by becoming 156. Between 1963 and 1970, over 400 similar coaches were built. Its owner had brought this fine 36ft. coach many miles to attend this very special day.
(Copyright Norman Fairhead)

This Bristol LSX4G is well known in East Anglia bus preservation circles and was certainly very welcome at the Open Day. Completed in June 1950, ECOC LL744 (MAH744) was the second Bristol LS prototype built and carries body 4255. Fitted with an underfloor Gardner 4HLW engine, this 42 seat Light Saloon remained in service until 1972 and can normally be found residing at the Ipswich Transport Museum.
(Copyright Norman Fairhead)

New to Westcliff-on-Sea in 1939, AJN825, a Bristol K5G with body 6339 configured as L27/26R, remained in service until 1960 when it was withdrawn from service as Eastern National 1269. AJN825 has in recent years carried First Essex fleet numbers 90231 and 9001. This historic bus is seen here on the memorable ECW Open Day in 1985. *(Copyright Norman Fairhead)*

Development of new designs did not stop in spite of the war time restrictions. In 1944, the prototype of the post war Bristol K type with lowbridge bodywork was unveiled. This lowbridge was delivered to Eastern National in January 1944 and today this bus, 1274 (JVW430), is in the care of the Eastern National Preservation Group. Due to changes in the operators fleet numbering scheme JVW430 also carried the numbers 3885 and 2201. This fine Bristol is seen here at the ECW Open Day before the arrival of the crowds. *(Copyright Norman Fairhead)*

Two more vehicles previously in the Eastern National fleet attended the factory for the 20th July 1985 event. On the left is Eastern National 1107(ONO49), a 1949 Bristol L5G bus, and on the right is Eastern National 331(7017HK), a 39 seat Bristol MW6G coach completed in July 1958 with body 10145. *(Copyright Norman Fairhead)*

With over 5000 Bristol Lodekka bodies built at ECW it was essential that at least one example attended the Open Day. This was admirably covered by ECOC LFL57 (BNG557), which was completed at the factory in December 1962.
Originally fitted with a Bristol engine, this 30ft. long Bristol FL6G carries body 13120 configured as H38/32R on chassis 198.002. Illuminated advertising panels are fitted to LFL57 and these can be seen in this view. LFL57 is normally in residence at the East Anglia Transport Museum.
(Copyright Norman Fairhead)

It was an unexpected surprise on 21st May 1986, when Bristol MW6G registration 56GUO, owned by Fareline Coach Services, turned up at the factory to collect spare parts. This coach was completed in June 1961 as Western National 2267 and has chassis 184.046 and body 12240 in C39F configuration. Whilst owned by Western National, 2267 spent time on loan to Alder Valley and Crosville. Usually mounted on Bristol chassis, this body design was also used on other makes of chassis such as AEC. (Copyright Norman Fairhead)

At one time Colchester Borough Transport had a large number of ECW bodied single and double deck buses in their fleet. Over 30 of the double deck buses were Leyland Atlanteans delivered between 1975 and 1980. By May 1997, Atlanteans in service had dropped to 21, one of which was open top. Colchester 68 (TPU68R) is one of those supplied by ECW to Colchester and is seen here at the factory on 12th April 1986 whilst visiting for repainting. This bus had body 22322 configured as H43/31F and was new in May 1977. (Copyright Norman Fairhead)

Former London Transport Guy Special 42 (MXX342) visited the factory on 31st October 1986. Completed in November 1953 with body 6382, this was one of 84 supplied to London Transport with B26F body work.

These smart and much admired little buses were designed by London Transport and powered by a Perkins P6 diesel. Having entered service in December 1953, during its life GS42 operated from Amersham, Dorking, Garston, Hemel Hempstead and Windsor garages. It was withdrawn in April 1972 and sold to a school via a dealer, after which GS42 passed into preservation. Behind GS42 is the large ECW store building. *(Copyright Norman Fairhead)*

This Bristol FLF6B was a feature of the chassis park for many months during 1986. The privately owned and some what neglected JHW68E arrived at ECW for work to be carried out there but nothing happened, and it remained in the chassis park and eventually left. Completed as Bristol Omnibus C7300 with H38/32F bodywork in February 1967, it has body 16103 on chassis 231.303. *(Copyright Norman Fairhead)*

Top Left - A view inside the factory on the 1985 Open Day showing a London Transport Leyland National bus on the Hywema lifts. This was one of 37 London Transport vehicles sent to ECW for refurbishment. London Transport was reported as stating they were very impressed with the quality and turn round time of the work. ECW built one Leyland National which was completed in April 1973 as Development Project C27, with the body being designated EX13. This National was first registered in 1980 and has been preserved. It is in use as a motor caravan and has apparently made several return trips to Spain. *(Copyright J. & F. Shipley)*

Top Right, Bottom Right - Two Leyland/DAB "bendibus" type vehicles are seen here at ECW when they visited the factory in 1984 for attention and appraisal. South Yorkshire PTE ordered thirteen of these vehicles for use in Sheffield. They were designed to carry 61 seated passengers and 73 standing. The great majority of the components used to build these vehicles were British, with some being made at ECW. DAB was a Leyland Danish subsidiary. *(Copyright J. & F. Shipley)*
Bottom Left - The interior of the Leyland/DAB "bendibus". *(Copyright J. & F. Shipley)*

Vehicles at the Factory - New

United body 402 and Daimler CB chassis 2047 were used in the building of United C72 (PW104) which is seen here when new in 1923 outside the front of the factory in Laundry Lane. Some C class models with Daimler CB chassis were built with rigid bodies, but C72 had a chara-bus body that seated 26 passengers. The solid tyres are probably due for early replacement since the high mudguards giving considerable clearances seem to indicate that the design allows for conversion to pneumatic tyres.
(Geoffrey Moore Collection)

United B35 (AH8099) was completed in 1922 and comprised of
White chassis 49177 with body 361 configured as B14F. The vehicle
is fitted with pneumatic tyres.
(Past Times Prints)

A scene inside the Body Shop in the early 1920s with a "Norfolk"
type body under construction and perhaps destined to be
mounted on the chassis in the foreground
(Malcolm White Collection)

A Gilford chassis 25 seat coach with United bodywork as supplied
to Orange Bros. of Bedlington in 1928.
(Malcolm White Collection)

Crosville 640(FM6911) is seen parked on the apron at the front of
the factory in 1932. This was one of five similar vehicles completed in
May 1932 and comprised body 2600 and Leyland TS4 chassis 109.
(Past Times Prints)

An impressive line up of twelve Western National Dennis Ace saloons and two unidentified others in March 1934. This view is looking west towards the railway crossing. These Western National Aces 706-717 (OD7795-7806) have bodies 3147-58 configured as B20F. In just over two years the name Eastern Counties on the building would be replaced by Eastern Coach Works. (*ECW*)

An equally impressive view of the factory from the railway crossing in May 1937, with nine newly completed single deck buses. Nearest, are four 32 seat Yorkshire Traction saloons with bodies 4884-7 mounted on Leyland Tiger TS7 chassis. Next, are three Westcliff-on-Sea Bristol JO5G saloons followed by Western Welsh and Eastern National saloons. The name of the new owner has already appeared on the building. (*ECW*)

An example of ECW excellence. It is 1953 and completed Red & White UC953 (LAX649) with body configured as C39F is ready to leave the factory. This Bristol LS comprised chassis 97.064 and body 6995 and was in service with Red & White from 1953 until 1969, after which it joined the fleet of Jones Omnibus Co. Ltd. of Aberbeeg. Later in life, LAX649 passed to a construction firm. *(Copyright Phillip Burcham)*

In total, Red & White took delivery of 55 Bristol LS vehicles of which 40 were buses. This particular 45 seat bus, U1554 (MAX115), was completed in August 1954 with body 6912 on chassis 101.144 and is seen here waiting to leave ECW to join the owner's fleet. The head office of Red & White was in Chepstow. *(Copyright Phillip Burcham)*

ECOC LL882 (XPW882X) was one of well over 100 coaches in the 1982 build programme. With a C47F body, it is seen here with "National" branding at the front of the factory during August 1982. The body was 25376 and the chassis used was Leyland Leopard PSU3G/4R 8131654. This new body design was given the Leyland Code B51. *(Copyright Robert Ranger)*

Lincolnshire 1455 (AVL744X) had a similar B51 body to the coach in the previous photograph and is seen here with "National" branding standing in Eastern Way in April 1982. It soon became apparent, after the early vehicles had been in service for a short while, that this design suffered from structural problems. The body on 1455 was 25084 and the chassis used was PSU3G/4R 8130911. *(Copyright Robert Ranger)*

The B51 body was also used on the Leyland Tiger TRCTL11/2R chassis, an example of which is seen here. London County TL19 (WPH119Y) was completed in August 1982 with body 25422 in C49F configuration. The coach, complete with tiger emblem, is in front of the factory with one of the many Ribble Olympians built at ECW behind. TL19 was one of an order for 42 similar coaches for London County intended for Green Line services.
(Copyright Robert Ranger)

Another of the London County coaches, TL5 (TPC105X), stands at the front of the factory in Eastern Way in July 1982, this time with the familiar "KEEP OUT" notice on the windscreen, signifying that the vehicle is now ready for delivery. TL5 comprised body 25408 configured as C49F and Leyland chassis TRCTL11/2R 8103203. After service with London County, this coach saw service with South Wales operator Davies of Pencader.
(Copyright Malcolm White/M. Hampson)

A comprehensive scene at the front of the factory on 19th August 1982 showing a 77 seat Olympian bus and two B51 bodied coaches. The Olympian is unregistered Ribble 2130 with body 25242, one of hundreds supplied with ECW body work to numerous operators. This particular bus was one of seven completed for Ribble between May and August in 1982 and was later registered VRN830Y. The chassis was ONLXB/1R ON418. On the left is 47 seat ECOC LL882 (XPW882X) and on the right is 53 seat Green Line TL36 (WPH136Y) the chassis of which was Tiger TRCTL11/2R 8200387. *(Copyright Robert Ranger)*

Perhaps more appropriate in the "Visiting" photographic section of this book, but nevertheless a new vehicle, this Leyland Royal Tiger Doyen demonstrator was at the factory for the open day in July 1985. Coaches of this type, some of which had bodywork built at the Charles H. Roe vehicle body building plant, visited ECW for warranty attention after the Roe factory had been closed in 1984 by Leyland. These coaches were later built at Leyland plants. *(Copyright Robert Ranger)*

During the Open Day, Ribble Motor Services 2171(C171ECK), an Olympian with body 26090 configured as CH42/30F, was used to demonstrate how a stability test was carried out on a double deck bus. Traditionally, for a stability test the bus was tilted to 28° with a full load of fuel, each upper deck seat loaded with 140 lbs., and the driver and conductor in their appropriate positions. For single deck vehicles different parameters applied.

A few days after being used in the demonstration, 2171 left the factory to start a working life in the north west of England. The head office of Ribble Motor Services, a former BET Group company, was in Preston.

(Copyright-Top Photograph Robert Ranger, Bottom Photograph Norman Fairhead)

During the last few years before Leyland closed the plant, a number of demonstration bodies and several small orders for bodywork on specialised vehicles were completed at ECW, in addition to many orders for conventional body work. A tri-axle double deck body mounted on an Olympian chassis and intended for the China Motor Bus Company is seen here under construction.
(*Copyright Robert Ranger*)

Hong Kong Citybus C52 is seen here at the 1985 Open Day awaiting the thousands of visitors who were able to sample the excellence of this Lowestoft built product that could seat 77 passengers in luxury. C52 was withdrawn from service in 1997 carrying the fleet number C103 having been renumbered a few years before. The body on this coach was 26237 and the chassis was ONLXCT/3RSp ON1711, it was one of two completed in 1985. A third was supplied but this was an upgraded 1982 demonstrator.
(*Copyright Norman Fairhead*)

The registration of the Olympian demonstrator was A33MRN, and with body 25762 it is seen here at the factory in early 1984 with an incorrect registration. During December 1985 this dual purpose vehicle passed to Preston Borough Council's fleet where it became their No. 3, this later changing to 33. The London Transport Leyland National buses on the extreme left are at ECW for refurbishment.
(Copyright Norman Fairhead)

At the 1985 Open Day, a large number of vehicles were on display with bodywork in various stages of completion. One of these was an almost complete Olympian for Metrobus of Orpington. This bus comprised body 26249 configured as H43/34F on chassis ONLXB/1R ON1938.
C395DML left the factory for delivery to Metrobus in August 1985. Established in 1983, this operator was taken over in 1999 by the Go-Ahead Group.
(Copyright Robert Ranger)

A description for this coach could be "simply the best", for at the 1984 British International Motor Show (IBCAM) it won the gold medal for excellence in design and workmanship beating all other competition at the show. The body of this Olympian coach was EX26 and although built for Ebdon's of Sidcup, they did not take delivery of it, and this award winner was eventually sold to South Yorkshire PTE in August 1986. This scene was recorded in October 1984.
(Copyright Norman Fairhead)

With such a large number of buses being built at ECW for London, it seemed at one point that the factory belonged to London Buses rather than Leyland. One example is seen here ready to leave ECW for London in May 1986. L78 (C78CHM) comprised body 26390 on chassis ONLXB/1RH ON2360 and seated 70 passengers. It was withdrawn from service in London in December 2003 and put into store. During April 2004, L78 was sold to Ensign Bus, Purfleet
(Copyright Norman Fairhead)

A SMALL SELECTION OF OTHER NEW VEHICLES

(All photographs copyright Norman Fairhead)

Body No. 25988   November 1984
Lothian Regional Transport 757(B757GSC)   Body Layout B51/32D
                Leyland Chassis ONTL11/2R ON1529

Body No. 26206   March 1985
London Country LRC6 (B106LPH)   Body Layout CH45/24F
                Leyland Chassis ONTL11/2RSp ON1712

Body No. 26191   22nd January 1985
Maidstone & District 5447(B447WKE)   Body Layout CH45/28F
                Leyland Chassis ONTL11/2RSp ON1693

Body No. 26453   August 1986
Reading Transport 81(D81UTF)   Body Layout CH39/27F
                Leyland Chassis ONLXCT/1RH ON10192

A SMALL SELECTION OF OTHER NEW VEHICLES

(All photographs copyright Norman Fairhead)

Body No. 26189   January 1985
Thames Valley & Aldershot 1510(B578LPE)   Body Layout CH45/28F
Leyland Chassis ONTL11/2RSp ON1708

Body No. 26211   9th July 1985
Eastern National 4500(B688BPU)   Body Layout CH45/28F
Leyland Chassis ONTL11/2RSp ON1766

Body No. 26553   March 1986
Eastern National 4017(C417HJN)   Body Layout CH42/30F
Leyland Chassis ONLXB/1RH ON10012

Body No. EX32 (For USA/Canada)   21st August 1984
Leyland/ Gillig --- (B757UHG)   Body Layout H39/29D
Leyland Chassis ONTL11/2L ON1410

A SMALL SELECTION OF OTHER NEW VEHICLES

(All photographs copyright Norman Fairhead)

Body No. EX36 (Body not built at ECW)
United 1500(B500MPY)

August 1984
Body Layout B46F

Leyland/DAB Chassis
Undergoing 30° Coach Stability Test at ECW

A SMALL SELECTION OF OTHER NEW VEHICLES

(All photographs copyright Norman Fairhead unless shown otherwise)

Body No. 26379   20th May 1986
Maidstone & District 5452(C452GKE)   Body Layout CH45/28F
Leyland Chassis ONTL11/2R ON10107

Body No. 26418   July 1986
Eastern National 4511(D511PPU/C511HJN)   Body Layout CH45/28F
Leyland Chassis ONTL11/2RH ON10077

Body No. 26379 (Upper Deck)   May 1986
Maidstone & District 5452(C452GKE)   Body Layout CH45/28F
Leyland Chassis ONTL11/2R ON10107 *(Copyright J. & F. Shipley)*

Body No. 26414   August 1986
Alder Valley North 1622 (D822UTF)   Body Layout CH39/21F
Leyland Chassis ONLXB/1RH ON10126

A SMALL SELECTION OF OTHER NEW VEHICLES

(All photographs copyright Norman Fairhead)

Body No. 26507   October 1986
London Buses L182 (D182FYM)   Body Layout H42/26D
Leyland Chassis ONLXB/1RH ON2509

Body No. 26374   June 1986
London County LRC11 (C211UPD)   Body Layout CH45/24F
Leyland Chassis ONTL11/2RSp ON10123

Body No. 26207   March 1985
London County LRC7 (B107LPH)   Body Layout CH45/24F
Leyland Chassis ONTL11/2RSp ON1713

Body No. 26376   June 1986
London County LRC13 (C213UPD)   Body Layout CH45/24F
Leyland Chassis ONTL11/2RSp ON10125

Body No. 26354 (For San Francisco, USA)   June 1986
Grosvenor Bus Lines Inc. 603 (2W98509)   Body Layout CH54/28D
Leyland Chassis ONCL10/2LVSp ON10081

Body No. 26360 (For San Francisco, USA)   July 1986
Grosvenor Bus Lines, Inc. 609 (2W98572)   Body Layout CH54/28D
Leyland Chassis ONCL10/2LVSp ON10087

A SMALL SELECTION OF OTHER NEW VEHICLES

(All photographs copyright Norman Fairhead)

Body No. EX25   January 1984
Leyland Demonstrator (Various Countries)   Body Layout H??/??D
                    Leyland Chassis ON----/-L ON1238

Body No. EX19 (26236)   1982 (Rebuilt 1985)
Demonstrator (Sold to Hong Kong City Bus)   Body Layout CH49/22D
                    Leyland Chassis ONLXCT/2R ON332

Body No. 26242   February 1985
Leyland Demonstrator (Indonesia)   Body Layout CH49/22D
                    Leyland Chassis ONTL11/3R ON1802

Body No. 26452, unknown, 26454   24th August 1986
Reading 80, Colchester, Reading 82   Various Body Layouts
                    Various Leyland ONLXC Chassis

A SMALL SELECTION OF OTHER NEW VEHICLES

Body No. 26452, unknown, 26454, 26360   24th August 1986
Reading 80, Colchester, Reading 82, Gray Line 609   Various Body Layouts
Various Leyland ON Chassis

Above and Bottom Left
Body No. 26600 (Final body)   January 1987
London Buses L263 (D263FUL)   Body Layout CH42/26D
Leyland Chassis ONLXB/1RH ON2645

On the Road

This unusual scene in June 1923, shows United A123 in Yarmouth Road at Lowestoft setting off for Great Yarmouth to participate in the Carnival there, with most of the passengers suitably dressed for the occasion. In usual United style, the fleet number is displayed on the side of the engine bonnet.
(Peter Killby Collection)

Another Lowestoft scene, this time at the Central railway station, showing two United single deck vehicles at work. The bus on the left is probably an "E" class, waiting to leave with a Service 4 to Kessingland. The overhead wires of the Lowestoft Corporation tramway are visible in this print.
(Past Time Prints)

Two West Yorkshire Road Car Co. Ltd. single deck buses share this delightful scene whilst employed on a private charter. On the left is Bristol L5G SG81 (DWW595) with body 6740 built in 1940, whilst on the right is a similar bus SG32 (CWY971) with body 6212 built in 1938. With bright paintwork, it appears that SG81 could be almost new when recorded at this stop-over. Both body numbers stated here are from ECW Series One. At one time, SG81 was West Yorkshire 190 and SG32 was 144. *(Allan Woods Collection)*

Top Left - In March 1933, ECOC A206 (NG3867) was completed at the Laundry Lane ECOC Bus Factory with a L30/26R body and joined their own fleet. This Leyland Titan TD2 originally had body 2873 but was later rebodied and is seen here with the later body heading for Norwich Bus Station in Queen's Road, Norwich. *(Copyright David Bowen)* **Top Right** - A batch of Leyland Titan TD1 double deckers with L28/24R bodies were completed in January 1931 at the factory for the ECOC fleet. One of the batch, A183 (NG1918) is seen here at Norwich Bus Station. This bus had body 2646 on Leyland chassis 72346. *(Copyright David Bowen)* **Bottom Left** - Lowestoft Corporation 10 (RT7723) was one of eight buses supplied to the local transport undertaking in 1931. It is seen here in the late 1930s passing through floodwater in London Road South. No. 10 was fitted with body 2559 and had chassis 6611542. Withdrawn from service in 1947, it was then sold to the London Brick Company who used it until 1952, after which it was broken up. *(Malcolm White Collection)* **Bottom Right** - Completed at ECOC in May 1934, Crosville 922 (FM8155) comprised body 3138 configured as L27/26R carried on Leyland TD3 chassis 4262. In 1935, 922 became M8 in the Crosville fleet and in the late 1940s received the new ECW body that is seen in this print. By the end of 1957, M8 had been withdrawn from service. *(Allan Woods Collection)*

Left - Cheltenham 91 (UHY375) was a Bristol KSW6G with body 7851 configured as H33/27R on chassis 106.006 and was one of four supplied in 1955/56 to Cheltenham & District. This scene was recorded on 7th October 1973 at Cheltenham. **Right** - Thames Valley 446 (DBL154) is a 1946 Bristol K fitted with an ECW 55 seat body and a 6 cylinder AEC 7.7 litre engine. It has been in preservation for many years. *(Both photographs copyright Malcolm White/Alan Robinson)*

Top Left - Another scene from 1973 showing 1955 built Cheltenham & District 91 (UHY375) this time working a service to Coronation Square in Cheltenham. *(Copyright Malcolm White/Graham Smith)* **Top Right** - Thames Valley 519 (EJB241) was completed in 1949 with a 55 seat ECW lowbridge body and is seen here after disposal by that operator and in use by a church. The engine of this Bristol K6B was the AVW, an engine also found in other buses including the L series. Thames Valley Traction Co. Ltd. was formed in 1920 although the ancestry of the company dates back to 1915 at Reading, as a branch of BAT. *(Copyright Malcolm White/Chris Riley)* **Bottom Left** - Lowestoft Corporation Transport 27 (GBJ198), was one of nine double deck buses supplied to the local council in 1947 with ECW H30/26R bodies mounted on AEC Regent II chassis powered by AEC 7.7 litre engines. It was more common to find this body design mounted on Bristol K series vehicles and these buses were something of a rarity. One of the nine, 21 (GBJ192), has been fully restored and can usually be found at the East Anglia Transport Museum. *(Malcolm White Collection)* **Bottom Right** - Cumberland Motor Services 291 (BRM596) was completed in 1936 and comprised a Massey body mounted on a Leyland TD4 chassis. It received a new ECW body in 1950 and, having spent many years with Cumberland, 291 was sold to Barton in 1959 and used by them until 1965 when it was withdrawn from service and sold for preservation. This scene was recorded on 20th August 1978. *(Copyright Malcolm White/Alan Robinson)*

Top Left - Western National 1611 (GDV460N), Southern National 1976 (464FTT) and Western National 2083 (BDV262C) make an interesting trio of ECW bodied buses and also gives the opportunity to compare the difference in the frontal appearance of the two 70 seat double deck Bristol FLF6Gs. Western National 1611 comprises 43 seat body 21317 and chassis LH6L LH-971 and at the time of writing (2007) remains in service in Malta carrying the registration EBY544. New in June 1961, Southern National 1976 had body 11748 and chassis 169.019 whilst Western National 2083 was new in March 1965 and carried body 15066 on chassis 224.167. **Top Right** - New in January 1958 and seen here at work in Cornwall, Western National 1938 (VDV755) was a Bristol LD6G carrying body 9580 on chassis 134.141. **Bottom Left** - In the very picturesque town of Dartmouth we find Western National 2028 (408PTA), a Bristol FLF6B at work. New in December 1963, 2028 had body 14043 on chassis 217.073; in 1976 it was sold and exported to the USA, where at one time, it was based in Denver, Colorado. **Bottom Right** - Hants & Dorset 1165 (HLJ22), a Bristol K6A with an ECW L27/28R body is seen here in the 1950s at Bournemouth. Entering service in late 1948, 1165 was fitted with an AEC 7.7 litre engine and in 1965 was withdrawn from service. At one time 1165 had the fleet designation TD873. Hants & Dorset Motor Services Ltd. commenced services at Bournemouth in 1916 and just visible in this view are the overhead wires of the trolley bus system there.
(All photographs from the Allan Wood Collection)

Top Left - At the end of their service lives, many buses are broken up whilst others are found different uses. This 1936 Dennis Ace carries ECW body 3311 and was at one time West Yorkshire 116 (YG5738). It is seen here amongst the depot weeds in use as a stores van. Perhaps the subject of this print should be compared with images of Aces found elsewhere in this book. **Top Right** - Unlike previous coach designs that were generally based on adapted bus bodies, the ECW 27ft. 6ins. x 7ft. 6ins. coach body introduced in 1950 was a complete change with a full fronted design and individual style. West Yorkshire Road Car SB13 (JWU891) was an example of this design being built in 1950 and comprising a Bristol L6B chassis and FC31F body. **Bottom Left** - Bristol Omnibus 2385 (LHT903) was a Bristol L6B new in 1948 and had a B35R body. Withdrawn by Bristol Omnibus in 1962 it passed to a dealer who then sold it to AA Motor Services (Dodds of Troon). In 1968, this bus passed to a builder. **Bottom Right** - The 1950 ECW coach design was revised and in 1951 a 30ft. x 8ft. version appeared with modified front styling and revised body details. Former Lincolnshire Road Car 2055 (HBE509) carried a FC35F body mounted on a Bristol LWL6B chassis and is seen here following disposal, in use as a school owned bus. *(All photographs from the Allan Wood Collection)*

An unusual colour for an ECW bodied Bristol K6B, but after service with Bristol Tramways and Carriage Company (BTCC) as their C3440, LHY929 saw service as a staff bus with West Country company Brains (Food Products) Ltd. C3440 entered service in 1949 with a H31/28R body. This view was recorded at a rally in June 1984 and includes another former BTCC Bristol K with an ECW body that is now preserved in the Bristol Omnibus Vehicle Collection. This bus, BOC 8336 (UHY384), is a 1955 KSW6G with a H33/27R body.
(Copyright Malcolm White/Cliff Essex)

Hants & Dorset fleet No. 1245 (JEL264) was a Bristol K6B with an ECW L27/28R body and entered service in 1950. It was withdrawn from service by Hants & Dorset in 1967 and is seen here later at work with operator Jones of Llandeilo, Carmarthenshire.
(Copyright Malcolm White/C. Keal)

In 1953, eighty four bodies were built at ECW for London Transport to be mounted on Guy "Special" (GS) chassis. These well liked small buses with bodies configured as B26F and painted in Lincoln Green were designed by London Transport. They were intended for one man operation on light loading routes, or where the roads were perhaps unable to cope with larger vehicles. Many of the 84 are now preserved. **Top Left** - A fine print showing Guy Special 21 (MXX321) at Orpington in 1957 whilst based at Dunton Green. This GS had body 6369 and was scrapped in 1972. (*Allan Woods Collection*) **Top Right** - Guy Special 66(MXX366) with body 6413 is captured here working route 448 which it operated whilst based at Guildford. GS66 was scrapped in 1973. (*Allan Woods Collection*) **Bottom Left** - Two ECW bodied Hants & Dorset vehicles are seen here at Winchester in the 1950s. On the left is 690 (KEL733), a Bristol AVW powered LWL6B built in 1951, and carrying an ECW FC35F body. On the right is 1122 (GLJ965), a Gardner 5LW powered Bristol K with a L27/28R lowbridge body. Withdrawn in 1965, this bus was at one time Hants & Dorset 788. (*Allan Woods Collection*) **Bottom Right** - Over 320 Bristol SC single deck buses were bodied by ECW and Cumberland had just twelve of these, five of which were new. Cumberland 403 (XAO611) was one of the new vehicles and is seen here at Whitehaven. One of two completed in June 1959, 403 left ECW with a C33F body and was the only one of the five new Cumberland SCs classified as a coach. It had body 11354 carried on chassis SC4LK 147.026 and in 1961, 403 was renumbered 204. By the end of 1971, 204 had been withdrawn from service by Cumberland. (*All photographs from the Allan Wood Collection*)

At one time ECW bodied buses were a common sight in and around York and today the odd Olympian can still be seen there. Back in the 1960s and 70s various versions of the Bristol Lodekka could be found almost everywhere in the city. **Top Left** - A Bristol FS6B of York-West Yorkshire, 3794 (EWU875C), is seen at Heslington. Completed at ECW in February 1965, this bus had body 14837 configured as H33/27RD mounted on chassis 223.118. **Top Right** - A short distance from York Minster, in St. Leonards Place, two York-West Yorkshire buses pass on 17th March 1978. On the left is 3796 (GYG615C), a Bristol FS6B completed in August 1965 with body 14839 on chassis 228.006, while on the right is 3951 (DWU836H), a 1970 Bristol VRT Series 2 with body 18241. **Bottom Left** - Recorded near York Railway Station on 29th November 1980 at the end of the York- West Yorkshire "Farewell to the Lodekka" tour and now preserved at the Keighley Bus Museum is 3821 (NWU265D), a Bristol FS6B with body 15468 configured as H33/27RD on chassis 230.055. **Bottom Right** - On 31st December 1977, York-West Yorkshire 3831 (KWX968D), a Bristol FS6B completed at ECW in April 1966 with body 15461 was recorded in Howard Drive, Rawcliffe. The air inlets associated with the Cave Brown Cave heating system are evident in this view on either side of the destination box. Many ECW products were fitted with this heating system which was invented by Wing Commander Cave-Brown-Cave of Southampton University. (*All photographs from the Allan Wood collection*)

Top Left - This view of a Crosville Bristol Lodekka LD6B at Liverpool shows the curved cab windows, the generous destination displays, large radiator grill together and the twin steps either side of the front number plate that were provided on this early Lodekka design. Completed at ECW in 1955 with a H33/25RD body, this bus carried the fleet designation ML767 until 1958 when it became DLB767(VFM632) in the Crosville fleet. (*Allan Woods Collection*) **Top Right**- The lower deck interior of an early Lodekka, similar to that of DLB767. The seating provided for five rear facing passengers can be seen on the front bulkhead as can the box structures enclosing the wheels in front of the inward facing seats in the foreground. (*ECW*) **Bottom Left** - Midland Red 440 (JOX 440P) was one of a pair completed by ECW in March 1976. The body was 21474, configured as H43/31F, and the chassis was Daimler Fleetline CRG6 67778. (*Allan Woods Collection*) **Bottom Right** - Completed at ECW in July 1962 with body 12885 as Western National 421(271KTA), this Bristol SUL4A has had a very interesting life. In 1969 it was converted from C33F configuration to DP33F and in 1979 to C37F. It was allocated to five different Western National depots before being sold and then served with five different operators, including Guernseybus, before passing into preservation. Chassis 190.036 was used for 271KTA, which is seen here whilst serving in the Memory Lane fleet as their "Lyn". (*Malcolm White Collection*)

Left - Western National 353 (FTT704), a Bristol K6A, is owned and cared for by the Bristol Vintage Bus Group. New in 1945, 353 originally had a Strachan lowbridge utility body; however in 1955 this was removed and replaced by an ECW L27/28R body. At the same time the radiator was replaced and the chassis renovated. An ongoing programme of maintenance and restoration ensures this bus is always well presented. This scene was recorded in 21st May 1978 near Warrington Bank Quay. *(Copyright Malcolm White/Alan Robinson)*

Right - Thames Valley S335 (LJB335F) was one of eight RESL6G buses with B33D bodies supplied by ECW in March 1968. S335 had body 16391 carried on chassis RESL-5-126. Recorded on 14th February 1969, this view shows S335 at Reading. *(Copyright Malcolm White/Dave Lindsell)*

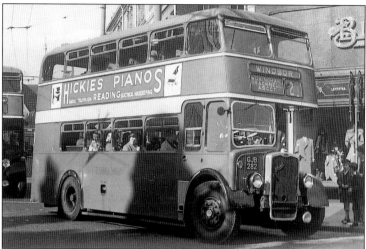

Top Left - Thames Valley 644 (GJB282) is seen here under the trolley bus wires at Reading. This Bristol KSW6B was powered by a 6 cylinder Bristol AVW engine and was completed in the early 1950s. It carried an ECW 55 seat lowbridge body. **Top Right** - Southern National 1849 (LTA992), a 1952 ECW bodied Bristol KSW6B was based at Weymouth for several years and is seen here at the depot there. **Bottom Left** - An attractive scene at Cambridge with two Bristol K series double deck buses passing. On the left is ECOC 301(MAH301), a 1951 Bristol KSW5G with a L27/28R body and on the right is ECOC 258 (KNG258), a 1950 Bristol K5G with a H30/26R body. **Bottom Right** - Skipton Road, Keighley in West Yorkshire is the location of this meeting of two Keighley - West Yorkshire ECW bodied buses. On the left is KDX165 (AWU467B), a Bristol FS6B completed in May 1964 with body 13874 configured as H33/27RD on chassis 214.163. In September 1983, KDX165 was exported to Florida, USA. On the right is KDB55 (HWW882), a Bristol K6B with a lowbridge 55 seat body. *(All photographs from the Allan Wood Collection)*

Top Left - Southern Vectis 866 (TDL566K) was one of seven Bristol RELL6Gs supplied to this Isle of Wight operator during the period between August 1971 and January 1972. The body supplied for 866 was 19350 and this was mounted on chassis RELL-3-1628. It is seen here at Ryde depot in 1985. *(Copyright Malcolm White/Martyn Davies)* **Top Right** - In early 1967, bodywork similar to that used on the Bristol RE chassis was supplied to West Hartlepool for mounting on five Leyland Leopard chassis. This order was rather special since they were the first Eastern Coachworks bodies supplied to an operator outside the State owned sector for many years. West Hartlepool Corporation 38 (EEF38D) with 42 seat body 16053 on Leyland L1 L63570 chassis was one of the five and is seen here on the left of this photograph. *(Copyright Malcolm White/Chris Riley)* **Bottom Left** - Leicester Corporation 126 (TRY126H) had B47D bodywork and entered service in March 1970. This RELL6L carried body 18112 on chassis RELL-3-942 and was one of 20 bodies supplied between December 1969 and March 1970. *(Copyright Malcolm White/Martyn Davies)* **Bottom Right** - During 1972, West Hartlepool was again a customer when an order for bodywork on Bristol RELL6L chassis was received. West Hartlepool 77 (OEF77K) was one of these and is seen here in the smart livery carried by Hartlepool buses that very much suited the successful and well liked RELL. This bus had body 19784 in B46D configuration carried on chassis RELL-3-1792 and entered service in August that year. It was one of seven supplied during July and August 1972. No. 77 was later converted for use as a mobile diner operated by Age Concern. *(Copyright Malcolm White/Alan Robinson)*

Top Left - Towyn Railway Station is the location of this meeting of two Crosville Bristol SC4LK single deck ECW bodied vehicles. On the left is CSG659 (908OFM) which was completed in May 1960 with body 12054 configured as C33F on chassis 158.020. This was one of 10 delivered to Crosville between May and July 1960. On the right is SC8 (341CFM), this had body 9020 on chassis 121.027 and was one of nine supplied to Crosville between July and October 1957. The body on SC8 was configured as B35F and in 1975 the fleet designation was changed to SSG608. Both CSG659 and SSG608 were withdrawn from service in 1975. CSG659 has the coach style radiator grill. **Top Right** - Buckden in the Yorkshire Dales is the location of this scene showing West Yorkshire CUG20 (OWX137) out on an excursion in this attractive area. One of 20 similar coaches in the West Yorkshire fleet, this Bristol LS6G with a C39F body was completed at ECW in May 1955. It was fitted with body 8256 mounted on chassis 107.039. **Bottom Left** - Another scene recorded at Buckden showing West Yorkshire 1373 (TWX195L) working a service to Skipton. This Bristol RELL6G had body 19113 configured as B53F mounted on chassis RELL-3-1836 and was new in December 1972. **Bottom Right** - In Devon, a classic pose for an ECW bodied Bristol RELL6G as Western National 2744 (TUO256J) works a service for Sidmouth. This RELL carried body 18527 on chassis RELL-3-1182 and could seat 53 passengers. *(All photographs from the Allan Wood Collection)*

Across the UK, perhaps the best known vehicles bodied by ECW will always be the Bristol Lodekka and the Bristol VR series of buses and coaches. An example of the Lodekka series is represented here by ECOC LFS101 (DNG401C) seen in Norwich on a private charter. This Bristol FS5G had body 14756 carried on chassis 223.112 and was completed in January 1965. It was one of 26 with H33/27RD bodywork delivered to ECOC between January and November 1965. After being withdrawn from service by ECOC, a period was spent in preservation in the UK followed by export to Poland in 1991. *(Copyright Norman Fairhead)*

Recorded in North Yorkshire, this print provides a contrast to the many town and city views in this book. The bus seen in this isolated location is West Yorkshire DX35 (OWX179), a Bristol LD6B with a H33/27RD body. Completed at ECW in March 1956 with body 8134 on chassis 116.032, it is working a York to Skipton service via Wetherby, Harrogate and Otley. *(Allan Wood Collection)*

Hants & Dorset 1387 (UEL708) is at Bournemouth waiting to leave with a service to Southampton. This Bristol LD6G with a H33/27R body was completed in August 1957 and comprised body 9406 on chassis 134.045. During September 1971, 1387 was renumbered 1451 in the Hants & Dorset fleet and in 1976 was withdrawn from service. *(Allan Wood Collection)*

Around York City

Top Left - Delivered from ECW with a H33/27RD body in August 1960, York - West Yorkshire YDX89 (2223WW) was a Bristol FS6B with body 11699 and chassis 155.075. York - West Yorkshire originates from 1934 when a committee was formed by York Corporation and West Yorkshire Road Car to run the former municipal services in York using West Yorkshire vehicles, at a time when the York Corporation tram and trolley bus services were abandoned. A similar scheme was set up in Keighley. **Top Right** - Outside York Railway Station we find West Riding 291(THL 254H), a Bristol RELL6G with a B53F body, one of 23 supplied between April and December 1970 to West Riding. This RELL had body 18636 mounted on chassis RELL-3-1031 and left ECW in April 1970 as West Riding 254. **Bottom Left** - West Yorkshire SRG45 (RYG604F), another Bristol RELL6G makes its way through the city streets. Completed at Lowestoft in September 1967, this RELL has body 16540 mounted on chassis RELL-3-188.
Bottom Right - Ten Bristol FS6B double deck buses with H33/27RD bodies were completed in March 1962 for West Yorkshire and York-West Yorkshire. One of these, York - West Yorkshire YDX130 (2029YG), is seen here passing York - West Yorkshire YSRG122 (JWU340J), a Bristol RESL6G with a B47F body which was completed in July 1971. YDX130 had body 12446 mounted on chassis 178.052 and YSRG122, had body 19561 and chassis RESL-8-236. *(All photographs from the Allan Wood Collection)*

In 1958, ECW supplied the bodywork for two railbuses ordered by British Railways. Powered by a 112hp Gardner engine, the railbuses had a maximum speed of 55mph and were intended for use on country branch lines in Scotland. The bodies were 42ft. 7ins. length and the chassis were supplied by Bristol. The pair were finished in British Railways standard green livery but did not prove very reliable in service, and were withdrawn in 1966. In April 1959 the railbuses were allocated to the Lugton - Beith branch in Ayrshire where one of them is seen. Experimental numbers EX1 and EX2 were allocated to the railbuses by ECW. *(Copyright ColourRail)*

In 1979, an experimental number was also allocated to the body fitted to Leyland chassis B45/6LXB B45.01. This became known as EX14 and was the forerunner of those fitted to the Leyland Olympian. It had features found on other bodies then in production in the UK including the Bristol VRT. This vehicle was used as a test bed by Leyland until June 1983 when it was sold to Stevensons of Uttoxeter in whose ownership it is seen here.
(Copyright Malcolm White/Mark Hampson)

Top Left - ECOC VR386 (BNG447J) is seen here at Norwich Bus Station on 27th July 1978. This Bristol VRT was completed in June 1971 and had body 18876 mounted on chassis VRT/SL2/6G/193. It was scrapped in November 1986. **Top Right** - ECOC LM612 (CPW612B) is also seen at Norwich on 27th July 1978. This Bristol MW5G was completed in November 1964 with a B45F body and was one of 162 MWs operated by ECOC. After being withdrawn from service with ECOC, LM612 passed to Coltishall dealer Jordan. It carried body 14111 on chassis 213.206. **Bottom Left** - ECOC LS831 (APW831B) was a Bristol MW6G completed at ECW in May 1964 with body 14457 configured as C39F and chassis 213.162 and is seen here at Peterborough during the evening of 26th July 1978 with "National" branding. In 1980, LS831 passed to dealer Hartwood Exports (Machinery) Ltd. **Bottom Right** - Completed at ECW as Lincolnshire 2522 (AVL216C) in May 1965, this Bristol FLF6G with H38/32F body is seen here as ECOC FLF433 at Peterborough on 26th July 1978. This bus was transferred from Lincolnshire to ECOC in 1973 and carried body 14964 on chassis 224.126. Whilst owned by Lincolnshire, AVL216C was renumbered from 2522 to 2711. *(All photographs copyright Malcolm White/Alan Robinson)*

Thames Valley 836(UJB202), was a Bristol FLF6G with a CH37/28F body. It was completed in November 1960 and had body 11420 mounted on chassis 169.007. This was one of the five FLF6Gs supplied to Thames Valley in 1960 with a sliding entrance door and is seen here approaching London Victoria Coach Station. *(Copyright Malcolm White/Cliff Essex)*

During 1967, eighteen bodies with H45/27D body work were supplied to Coventry Corporation on Daimler Fleetline CRG6LX chassis. One of the eighteen, Coventry 24 (KWK24F) with body 16727 on chassis 62634 is seen here. All eighteen were rebuilt to H45/29F in 1973-74 and in April 1974 passed to West Midlands PTE when the 305 vehicles in the Corporation fleet passed to that Authority. *(Copyright Malcolm White/ Graham Smith)*

An attractive scene at the Bristol Rally in 1998 featuring three preserved ECW bodied coaches all in Royal Blue livery. On the left is Southern National 1297 (OTT96), a 1953 Bristol LS6G originally with a C41F body but converted to C39F in 1961. This was transferred to Western National in 1969 and was retired by them in April 1970; it then had a succession of owners and has been preserved since 1972. In the centre is Western National 1420 (EDV502D), a 1966 Bristol MW6G with a C39F body. Whilst in service with Western National this coach was based at Plymouth and also Weymouth, and was retired by them in 1978. It carries body 15763 mounted on chassis 225.134. On the right is Western National 2200 (OTT43), another 1953 Bristol LS6G with a C41F body converted to C39F by ECW in 1961. Taken out of service in May 1969, 2200 had two periods of working for other operators before passing into preservation in 1998. *(Malcolm White Collection)*

A visitor to the Bus Station at Bridport in the middle of the morning on 10th September 2001 would have found five ECW bodied Bristol VRT buses with H43/31F bodywork operated by Southern National there, two of which are seen here. On the left is 1159 (AFJ766T) with body 24119 mounted on chassis VRT/SL3/6LXB/1976 and on the right is 1163 (AFJ770T), with body 24123 on chassis VRT/SL3/6LXB/2003. When completed in November 1979, both buses were in Western National livery. These two were part of an order for 42 similar buses from Western National for delivery between August 1979 and May 1980. *(Copyright Malcolm White)*

Left - Scarborough and the North Yorkshire moors are regularly featured on national television and scenes often include preserved ECW bodied buses. The very popular resort of Scarborough has been well known for many years by enthusiasts for the interesting buses used on the extensive sea front services that run during the summer months around the North and South Bays. Sometimes referred to as the "coal barge", United 4278 (PHN178L), a Bristol RELL6G, was one of six completed at ECW between December 1972 and March 1973 with B50F bodies. In a much modified OB50F form, 4278 is seen here on 20th July 1996 in Westborough at Scarborough. This RELL has had several owners including Scarborough & District and East Yorkshire. **Right** - On the evening of 10th September 2001 at Portland Bill, First Southern National 934 (VDV134S) waits before returning to Weymouth. Completed at ECW in November 1977, 934 has often been used in open top mode. It was one of six that left ECW with CO43/31F bodies in November 1977 for Western National. The body carried by 934 is 22427 on chassis VRT/SL3/6LXB/1023. The Western National fleet of VRTs with CO43/31F bodies have carried ship names and 934 was "Golden Hind". *(Both photographs copyright Malcolm White)*

Left - Two ECW bodied buses are seen here on Scarborough sea front on 31st August 1997. On the left is Shoreline Suncruisers 4 (HPK507N), a Bristol VRT Series 2 that is well known in and around Scarborough. Originally this was Alder Valley 930. On the right is former Bristol Omnibus 8579 (869NHT), one of four supplied with CO33/27R bodies in November 1961. 869NHT was in service with Lincolnshire operator Applebys when this image was recorded. *(Copyright Malcolm White)*

Bottom Left - The London Bus Export Co. is another location often visited by enthusiasts. Seemingly hundreds of buses and coaches are to be found there, many of which are kept in a roadworthy condition. On the evening of 18th August 1996, OWJ637A, a Bristol LD6G with body 9328 converted to open top, stands outside the gates of this Lydney based company. This bus was completed in March 1958 as Crosville MG946 (928CFM) with a H33/27RD body and has also carried the registration ACA217A. *(Copyright Malcolm White)* **Bottom Right -** Last reported as being in San Diego, California having been exported in 1986, former Western SMT B2254 (OCS584H) is seen here in service as United 644 on 25th May 1980 at Scarborough. *(Copyright Malcolm White/Alan Robinson)*

Top Left - This Bristol LH6L with a B43F body entered service in 1978 as Bristol Omnibus 423 (SWS 769S) and was one of seven buses completed in June 1978 for Bristol Omnibus, the body being 23484 mounted on chassis LH-1494. Withdrawn by Bristol in 1983, SWS769S served with three other operators before being taken off the road and used for storage. This scene was recorded during the period 1997-2000 when it was owned by W. Appleby. *(Allan Wood Collection)* **Top Right** - At one time London Country had over 60 of the short ECW bodied Bristol LHS buses, one of which was BH55 (TPJ55S). This is shown here as South Yorkshire Transport 1051 in their City Nipper livery after being sold by London Country. Following use by South Yorkshire this bus passed to Busways Travel and was scrapped in 1995. *(Copyright Malcolm White/Chris Riley)* **Bottom Left** - A scene at Southampton on 11th October 1985 featuring Hampshire Bus 3846 (YAE518V). This Bristol LH6L entered service in late 1979 as Bristol Omnibus 451 and passed to Hants & Dorset in 1981 and Hampshire Bus in 1983. It also spent time with Musterphantom (Short Blue Line), Southern Vectis, Trimdon Motor Services, Teeside Motor Services, Appleby and Stephensons (Rochford). The body carried by this Leyland powered bus was 23529 on chassis LH-1586. *(Copyright Malcolm White/R. Price)* **Bottom Right** - Wilts & Dorset 3841 (YAE513V) was originally Bristol Omnibus 446 and in 1981 became Hants & Dorset 3841. In 1983, it became Wilts & Dorset 3841 and in 1993 passed to Damory Coaches. Recorded on 2nd August 1984, this view shows the cut away front of 3841; this allowed it to be used on the Sandbanks ferry. YAE513V was scrapped in 1999. *(Copyright Malcolm White/Alan Robinson)*

Top Left - Lowestoft Corporation was supplied with B45D bodywork for ten AEC Swift buses during 1969-73. One of the first four, 2 (YRT896H), is seen here at Gunton Estate in the north of the town after the Corporation run services passed to Waveney District Council . This bus had body 18061 carried on AEC chassis 2MP2R479. *(Malcolm White Collection)* **Top Right** - Fifty-three seat United Counties 311(NBD311F) was completed at ECW in January 1968 with body 16525 on chassis RELL-3-218. It was one of six supplied between November 1967 and May 1968 and is seen here as Luton & District 311. *(Copyright Malcolm White/Chris Riley)* **Bottom Left** - This Bristol RELH6L has had an eventful life having passed into preservation twice. Supplied to Bristol Omnibus with DP49F bodywork, it was one of eight completed during June and July 1970 for Bristol. After being sold in 1983 it passed to Cheltenham & Gloucester Omnibus and in 1985 into preservation. During 1986, WHW374H returned to public service after purchase by YC Travel followed by service with Easton's, Ward Smith and Pennine Blue. In June 1992 it was again purchased for preservation. Leyland powered WHW374H carries body 18766 on chassis RELH-4-306. *(Copyright Malcolm White/D. Badger)* **Bottom Right** - Western National/Royal Blue 2367 (HDV643E) was completed in March 1967 with C47F bodywork. This Bristol RELH6G carried body 16626 on chassis 238.047 and was one of six supplied to Western National and sister company Southern National during March 1967. *(Copyright Malcolm White/Alan Robinson)*

Top Left - National Travel West ordered four 53 seat coaches with Leyland chassis for delivery between November 1982 and April 1983 and one of the four, National Travel West 93 (ANA93Y), is seen here later in life as Eastern National CF1309. This coach had body 25450 carried on chassis PSU5E/4R 8230485 and is seen here at Chelmsford in 1987. *(Copyright Malcolm White/Cliff Essex)* **Top Right** - After being withdrawn from service by United this ECW bodied Bristol LS bus was sold to G. Stevenson and used for transporting staff. This scene was recorded in May 1976 and just visible is the very dirty front registration plate showing the vehicle registration to be VHN398. *(Copyright Malcolm White/Cliff Essex)* **Bottom Left** - Fifteen Bristol SC4LK thirty-five seat buses were supplied to ECOC between March 1957 and January 1958 with B35F bodies. One of these was ECOC LC544 (VVF544) which is seen here later in life at Colchester whilst in the fleet of W. Norfolk & Sons of Nayland. LC544 was sold by ECOC to dealer Jordan of Coltishall in 1971, and then passed into the Norfolk fleet where it remained until the end of 1972. It was then sold to a dealer who resold the bus in 1974 for scrap. *(Copyright Malcolm White/Chris Riley)* **Bottom Right** - One of many successful joint ventures between BCV and ECW, the Bristol SU was designed for use as a small capacity coach or bus. It was in production between 1960 and 1966 during which time two types of SU were produced, a short version, the SUS, and the longer SUL. Powered by an Albion 4 cylinder 4.1 Litre engine, the seating capacity for the SUS was 30 passengers. When completed as a bus the SUL could seat 36, while the coach version could seat 33. Seen here is Western National 671 (BDV252V), a SUL4A completed in 1965 with body 14720 carried on chassis 226.022. *(Copyright Malcolm White/R. Price)*

The end for this Gardner 6HLX powered Bristol RELH6G came in December 2000 when it was broken up for spares. Western National 1451(LDV469F) had body 17060 configured as C45F and carried on chassis ELH-4-134. It was one of eight completed at ECW between February and May 1968 for Western National and sister company Southern National and is seen here at Bridport in 1981 on a private charter. *(Copyright Malcolm White/Martyn Davies)*

Recorded at Salisbury in April 1977, Hants & Dorset 612 (RLJ798H) was a Bristol RELL6G with 45 seat bus body 17712 carried on chassis RELL-3- 833. It was completed at ECW as Wilts & Dorset 832 during November 1969 being one of seven supplied between June 1969 and February 1970. *(Copyright Malcolm White/R. Price)*

A scene at Toddington on the Gloucestershire Warwickshire Railway on 24th August 1996 showing preserved Cheltenham & District 1000 (KHW306E), a Bristol RELL6L and one of four delivered to that operator in June 1967. Withdrawn in 1981, 1000 passed to the Cheltenham Bus Preservation Group and then to the Birmingham & Midland Motor Omnibus Trust at Wythall. The body is 16462 in B53F configuration and the chassis is RELL-3-122. Standing next to 1000 is 72 (HDG448), a preserved Albion Venturer. *(Copyright Malcolm White)*

ECOC LL718 (KNG718), a Bristol LL5G with B39R bodywork is one of a number of vehicles with Bristol L series chassis that have been preserved. Completed at ECW in 1950, LL718 is seen here on 21st May 1978 near Warrington Bank Quay heading for the Burtonwood Rally. The Bristol L series is usually considered to be the single deck equivalent of the double deck Bristol K series.
(Copyright Malcolm White/Alan Robinson)

Top Left - Thirty five Daimler Fleetlines with H43/34F bodies were completed at ECW during 1971 for Scottish operator Central SMT. Seen here in service as the Eagle Community Bus after being sold by Central is one of the thirty five. This was originally Central SMT D28 (TGM228J) and carried body 18259 on chassis CRG6LX 64710. This scene was recorded in August 1990. *(Copyright Malcolm White/Cliff Essex)* **Top Right** - In early 1976, body work on ten Daimler Fleetline CRG6LX chassis was completed for Thamesdown. One of these, Thamesdown 176 (KMW176P) passed to Lincolnshire operator Applebys who used it as an open top bus at Scarborough. It carried body 20855 mounted on chassis 68734 and is seen here near the harbour whilst working a sea front service. *(Allan Wood Collection)* **Bottom Left** - Southdown received fifteen Daimler Fleetlines with H43/31F bodywork from ECW in May 1972. One of the fifteen is seen here as Crosville HDL922 (XUF392K) after passing to that operator in 1980. This had body 19705 mounted on chassis CRL6 65398 and when new was Southdown 392. Crosville HDL925, another of the Southdown fifteen, is on the left. This scene is at Warrington in 1980. *(Copyright Malcolm White/Chris Riley)*

A good view of Standerwick 69 (OCK69K) on 16th August 1972 turning into Gillingham St. Garage in Victoria. Completed in October 1971, this coach was one of thirty built for Standerwick in 1971- 72. The body was 18979 configured as CH42/18CT and when this design was unveiled it was reported as being the first 36ft. x 8ft. 2½ ins. double deck coach design to be built in this country. The prototype attended the Commercial Motor Show where it aroused much interest. In 1974, this coach passed to National Travel (West) and no longer exists. Gillingham Street garage was demolished in the late 1990s.
(Copyright Malcolm White/Chris Elkin)

Originally York-West Yorkshire 3719 (FWR216T), this Bristol VRT, was completed in June 1979 with H43/31F body work. It was acquired by Cambus from York City & District and is seen here leaving Drummer Street Bus Station in Cambridge as Cambus 730. In May 2001, 730 was scrapped, the last owner being Bailey of Hucknall. Body 23433 was supplied for 3719 carried on chassis VRT/SL3/6LXB/1891
(Copyright Malcolm White/Chris Riley)

Top Left - At the Grimsby depot of Lincolnshire Road Car on 21st May 1980 we find 1018 and 1653, two Bristol LH buses with ECW bodies. On the left is 1968 built 1018 (GVL909F) with body 17415 in DP41F configuration on chassis LH-144, and on the right is 1972 built 1653 (OVL452K) with body 19609 in B43F configuration on chassis LH-617.
(Copyright Malcolm White/Alan Robinson)

Centre Left - When an ECW special event is organised by the East Anglia Transport Museum the evening road run for vehicles is always interesting with a stop being made on Gunton Cliff, Lowestoft, a location with a long association with ECW, where three of the 2002 event participants are seen. On the right is a 49 seat coach that was completed in April 1975 as Greater Manchester Transport 81 (HNE641N). This has body 21499 mounted on Leyland Leopard PSU3B/4R chassis 7500131. Behind 81 is former West Yorkshire PTE 45 (MUA45P), a Bristol LHS with body 21585 configured as B27F on chassis LHS-242. This was new in July 1976. On the far left is a former Southdown 1946 built Leyland Tiger PS1. *(Copyright Malcolm White)*

Bottom Left - This Applebys coach was completed by ECW with a C49F body as City of Oxford 32 (VUD32X) in April 1982. The body was 25360 carried on Leyland chassis PSU3G/4R 8131664.
(Allan Wood Collection)

Looking superb in the Border Clipper livery, Cumberland 1001(URM801Y) with H45/32F bodywork was recorded at Carlisle in August 1988. Completed in November 1982, this Olympian has body 25123 carried on chassis ONLXB/1R ON397 and was originally Cumberland 801.
(Copyright Malcolm White/Cliff Essex)

Looking very smart in the corporate livery, Trent 706 (XCH706Y), was recorded at Derby in September 1984. Now in service with Blackpool Transport, this Olympian has body 25617 mounted on chassis ONLXB/1R ON614. The registration XAU706Y was at one time allocated to 706.
(Copyright Malcolm White/Alan Robinson)

Top Left - Southern Vectis 702 (CDL899), a Bristol K5G, was new in 1939 and comprised body 6462 configured as H30/26R on chassis 51100. In the late 1950s it was converted to open top and survives in that form today. This view of 702 was recorded at Sandown on the Isle of Wight in 1972. *(Copyright Malcolm White/Martyn Davies)* **Top Right** - This June 2006 view shows another open top bus on the Isle of Wight. This is Southern Vectis 683 (934BDL), a Bristol VRT and it is passing through Lake. *(Copyright Malcolm White/Martyn Davies)* **Bottom Left** - Completed in 1941 as Bristol Omnibus C3315 (GHT127) with a H30/26R body, this bus was rebuilt by Bristol Tramway & Carriage Co. in 1951 and in November 1955 passed to Brighton, Hove and District where it was converted to a permanent open top vehicle and became 992 in their fleet. In 1965, 992 was sold to a dealer who resold it to Thomas Bros. of Port Talbot. During December 1969, the bus was sold to Bristol Omnibus and is seen here in the Guide Friday livery. It is owned by First Group and is on long term loan to Bristol Vintage Bus Group. *(Copyright Malcolm White/Steve Powell)* **Bottom Right** - Preserved former Colchester Borough Transport 90 (RVW90W) was chartered by the local railway operator in July 2002 at the time of the Lowestoft air show and is seen here parked near Lowestoft Railway Station. This Leyland Atlantean AN68A/1R with body 23655 was completed in July 1980 with the H43/31F bodywork being carried on chassis AN68A/1R 7905774. *(Copyright Malcolm White)*

Another view of an ECW special event organised by the East Anglia Transport Museum showing some ECW bodied vehicles at the former factory site. This small sample of buses includes the following.
From left to right:- Bristol Lodekka, Bristol VRT, Bristol SUL4A [former West Yorkshire SMA5 (811BWR)], Leyland Olympian [former City of Oxford 224 (CUD224Y)], Bristol LH6L [former Devon General 112 (KTT42P)] and Leyland Olympian [Ipswich Buses 48(C97CHM)].
(Copyright Malcolm White)

A fine view of former United 6080 (SHN80L) at Carlton Colville on 13th July 2002. This Bristol RELH6G has DP49F bodywork and was one of twenty supplied to United between May and October 1973. Now preserved, 6080 was completed at ECW in July 1973 and carries body 20364 on chassis RELH-4-622.
(Copyright Malcolm White)

A visit to York on 17th October 2006 found Olympians with Lowestoft built bodies in service in the city centre. **Top** - First Group 30679 (A686MWX) is seen here in Station Rise at the bus stops outside the historic former headquarters of the North Eastern Railway and now the GNER headquarters. This Olympian was one of three remaining at York in 2006 with ECW H45/32F bodywork. It was new to York-West Yorkshire in January 1984 when it became 3835 in that fleet and has body 25856 carried on chassis ONLXB/1R ON1137. This image was recorded from the top of the city wall and since then, 30679 has passed into preservation in North Yorkshire. **Bottom** - Stephenson of Easingwold have Leyland Olympian JTY399X in their fleet. This coach hire firm runs a local bus service from York to Easingwold via Linton-on-Ouse and another from York to Kirkbymoorside via Easingwold, and undertakes school contract work. Depots are at Kirkbymoorside and Tholthorpe. JTY399X has body 25004 carried on chassis ONLXB/1R ON129 and was one of sixteen supplied to Northern General between November 1981 and January 1982 with H45/32F bodies. JTY399X was Northern General 3599 and is seen here in St. Leonard's Place in the city.
(Photographs copyright Malcolm White)

Ipswich Transport Museum held an ECOC rally in October 2006 and several ECW bodied vehicles were there including the following. **Top Left** - Bristol Tramways 2800 (NHU2), a Bristol LSX6G bus. This entered service with Bristol Tramways in 1950 and was retired from service in 1967 by Bristol Omnibus. In 1956, it was converted to LS5G. **Top Right** - ECOC LKH133 (HPW133), a Bristol K5G with H30/26R bodywork that can normally be found at the Lincolnshire Road Transport Museum. LKH133 was new in May 1949, and was initially loaned to London Transport to help with the bus shortage in London. **Bottom Right** - ECOC RE658 (KVF658E), a Bristol RESL6G with B46F bodywork. New in 1967 this bus has body 16350 carried on chassis RESL-1-118. Since 1982, RS658 has been owned by the Eastern Transport Collection.

(All photographs copyright Malcolm White)

In the 21st Century, a number of the 1218 ECW bodied Bristol LH single deck buses are still in front line public service. For the great majority including the two featured on this page, the days of serving the public on a daily basis as PSVs are over, with many now being scrapped. These two had different destinies after withdrawal from PSV use.

Top - Between November 1974 and February 1975, Hants & Dorset took delivery from ECW of twenty Bristol LH6L buses with B43F bodywork. Seen here is 3544 (GLJ476N), this was completed in November 1975 with body 21336 mounted on chassis LH-978. After withdrawal from service by Hants & Dorset, 3544 passed to a London based catering company. (Copyright Malcolm White/R. Price) **Bottom** - Completed in October 1975 as Western National 112 (KTT42P) with B43F bodywork, this Bristol LH6L had a period of ownership under Lincolnshire County Council and also the National Coal Board before being sold for preservation in 2000. It has body 21659 carried on chassis LH-1139 and is seen here in the livery carried when in service with Devon General. This was one of twenty supplied to Western National between July and October 1975.
(Copyright Malcolm White)

Three Leyland Olympians were completed for Eastern National during July 1986 with CH45/28F bodywork mounted on chassis ONTL11/2RHSp. One of these, 4510 (D510PPU) is seen here whilst visiting the East Anglia Transport Museum for a special ECW event on 13th July 2002 after being retired by Eastern National (Essex Buses Ltd.), and in the ownership of Sanders Coaches of Holt. This fine coach has body 26417 and more recently has been owned by Flagfinders of Braintree with a new registration of PLZ2876. Another ECW bodied Olympian, City of Oxford 224 (CUD224Y), is at the rear of the Sanders coach.
(Copyright Malcolm White)

Clydeside Buses 891 (C451BKM) was completed at ECW in September 1985 with body 26248 as Maidstone & District 5451 and is seen here in July 1996 at Buchanan Street Bus Station in Glasgow. The CH45/28F bodywork of this coach is carried on Leyland chassis ONTL11/2R ON 2023.
(Copyright Malcolm White/Cliff Essex)

A 1982 scene at Lowestoft Bus Station showing Eastern Counties VR221 (BVG221T) and the shelters before they were modernised. The body of VR221 was 23155 configured as H43/31F and carried on chassis VRT/SL3/6LXB/1565. This bus no longer exists having been scrapped in 1998.
(Malcolm White Collection)

Seven Leyland Olympians were delivered to Trent with H45/32F bodywork between March and June 1983. One of the seven is seen here in October 2006 as Blackpool Transport 403 (XAU703Y). This was originally Trent 703 and has body 25614 carried on chassis ONLXB/1R ON603.
(Copyright Malcolm White/Martyn Davies)

Top Left - The annual transport rally at Harmans Cross on the Swanage Railway is always well attended and has a good selection of vehicles. On 15th September 2002, former Southern National/Royal Blue 2278 (766MDV), a Bristol MW6G with C39F body work was present at the rally. This has body 13672 carried on chassis 204.091 and was new in May 1963. *(Copyright Malcolm White)*

Top Right - Dressed for a wedding, former Southern National/Royal Blue 2250(617DDV) is seen here in Kingston in September 2002. This Bristol MW6G has the C39F older design bodywork and was new in June 1960. It has body 11945 carried on chassis 164.034. *(Copyright Malcolm White/Cliff Essex)* **Bottom Right** - Open top buses have a limited but much appreciated role when used for special occasions. South Wales 500 (WNO484) has been fitted with a loudspeaker and illuminated signs to carry Father Christmas during the festive season. Formerly Eastern National 2386, a 1953 Bristol KSW5G with L27/28R bodywork, it was converted to O33/28R in the 1960s. *(Copyright Malcolm White/C. Keall)*

East Suffolk has two fine transport museums where examples of once familiar buses and coaches can be found. On special occasions visits by a number of vehicles currently in public service use are arranged.

Top - At the East Anglia Transport Museum on 8th July 2001, an ECOC Leyland Olympian with Lowestoft built bodywork was in attendance. This bus was completed at ECW in March 1983 as Trent 700 (XAU700Y) and one of seven supplied to that operator between March and June 1983. It has body 25611 mounted on chassis ONLXB/1R ON 597. *(Copyright Malcolm White)*

Bottom - On 1st October 2006, former ECOC Bristol VRT VR144 (GNG710N) was on display at the Ipswich Transport Museum. Now privately owned and preserved, VR144 has had the Silver Jubilee livery restored that was applied during December 1976. This livery is similar to that applied to the new Alder Valley Olympians; a photograph of one of these can be found on page 119. With body 20480 on chassis VRT/SL2/6G/933, VR144 entered service with ECOC in January 1975 and passed into preservation in 2003. *(Copyright Malcolm White)*

As might be expected, the majority of ECW bodied vehicles remaining in front line public service today (2007) are Leyland Olympians, the last type in large scale production at the factory. At the annual Lowestoft Air Show the railway is unable to cope with the numbers of travellers and buses have been brought in to help by the local train operator. In recent years, ECW bodied Olympians have been included in the fleet of buses chartered. Both those featured here have H45/32F body work.

Top - Carters Coach Services superbly painted Leyland Olympian C664LJR is seen leaving the railway station in the town during the air show. This is one of 45 delivered in 1985 to Northern General and carries body 26036 on chassis ONCL10/IRV ON1970. The red and white radio mast above the bus is that of a former pirate radio ship in the harbour. **Bottom** - Originally Ribble 2136 (DBV136Y), this Leyland Olympian was one of seven completed in May 1983 for Ribble and carries body 25623 on chassis ONLXB/IR ON 743. It is seen here in the station taxi area at Lowestoft station in Cedric's livery. Other operators to have had DBV136Y in their fleet include Arriva North West and Arriva Midlands North. *(Both photographs copyright Malcolm White)*

At the time of writing, Wilts & Dorset have over twenty ECW bodied Bristol VRT buses as front line service vehicles. Formed in 1915, Wilts & Dorset initially operated services around Salisbury and central Wiltshire. In 1972 the company merged with Hants & Dorset and in 1983 resumed its original identity with the break up of the NBC. During 2003, the company was acquired by the Go-Ahead group and now has a larger area of operation. Two of Wilts & Dorset Bristol VRTs are seen here, both were transferred from Hants & Dorset to Wilts & Dorset in 1983.

Top - Outside the classic stone built railway station at Swanage on 13th September 2001 we find 4426 (ELJ218V), a refurnished VRT that in early 2007 was allocated to Poole after earlier being at Salisbury. Completed in January 1980, 4426 has body 24094 carried on chassis VRT/SL3/6LXB/2100. The railway station is the headquarters of the Swanage Railway Co. and is only a short distance from the beach and shopping area. In addition to railway activities, it has a café, shops, large information centre and bus enquiry/booking office. The bus depot is nearby. *(Copyright Malcolm White)*
Bottom - Seen here with an overall advertisement, 3412 (BFX665T) was new in in March 1979 and carried body 23189 on chassis VRT/SL3/6LXB/1802. It was one of twenty delivered to Hants & Dorset between September 1978 and April 1979. In May 2005, 3412 was sold to a dealer for scrapping.
(Copyright Malcolm White/Mark Hampson)

West Riding took delivery of fourteen Bristol VRTs with standard H43/31F bodywork between November 1975 and May 1976, one of which was 762 (OWW906P) with body 21031 carried on chassis VRT/SL3/6LX/347. It is seen here in May 1980 specially painted in anniversary livery to celebrate 75 years of service by West Riding. Withdrawn from service in December 1987, 762 served with at least five other operators included Yorkshire Woollen and United Automobile Services before being sold for scrap in 1999.
(Copyright Malcolm White/Mark Hampson)

Almost at the end of its service life, First Eastern Counties Bristol VRT 263 (RAH263W) paid a visit to the East Anglia Transport Museum on 8th July 2001 on the occasion of a rally to celebrate 70 years of the Eastern Counties Omnibus Company. One of three delivered by ECW to ECOC with H43/31F body work during February 1981, 263 comprised body 24626 and chassis VRT/SL3/6LXB/2798.
The appearance of 263 at the rally with its authentic slightly worn rare livery was much appreciated by many enthusiasts. In April 2002, 263 passed to Coltishall dealer Jordan.
(Copyright Malcolm White)

This scene at Stoke-on-Trent adds to the already diverse range of vehicle fleets and locations that are included in this book. Potteries Motor Traction took delivery of ten Leyland Olympians with H45/32F bodywork between August and November 1983. The last of the ten to be completed, 742 (A742GFA) is seen here, this had body 25682 carried on chassis ONLXB/1R ON969. *(Copyright Malcolm White)*

Crosville Motor Services covered a large area that included North Wales and parts of Cheshire and was a long standing substantial customer of the Lowestoft factory. Crosville Wales EOG208 (C208GTU) is seen here with a striking Coastliner livery that includes a dragon. This Olympian was new in October 1985 with CH42/29F bodywork and was sold to ACE Travel of Aintree after being retired by Crosville. EOG208 was fitted with body 26074 on chassis ONLXB/1R ON2059 and was one of 32 supplied between December 1984 and October 1985, thirteen of which had the coach specification bodywork.
(Copyright Malcolm White/Chris Riley)

Top - A charming scene with a tree lined background that has similarities to the thousands of official ECW photographs taken in and around the park at Oulton Broad and Oulton village. This however is the East Anglia Transport Museum on 8th July 2001. On the **left** is First Blue Bus 325 (PVG25W), a Bristol VRT with H43/31F bodywork in the Great Yarmouth Borough Transport livery. New in February 1981, 325 comprised body 23460 and chassis VRT/SL3/6LXB/2839 and no longer exists having been scrapped. In the **centre** is former United Counties 712 (KBD712D), a 1966 Bristol FS6G with H33/27RD body work. This carries body 15435 on chassis 230.060. On the **right** is former United BGL29 (GHN189), a Bristol K5G new in 1942 and rebodied in 1954 at ECW with a 53 seat lowbridge body built five years earlier for a Leyland TD2. GHN189 has been preserved since 1970. *(Copyright Malcolm White)*

Bottom - Between March and May 1982, ten Olympians were supplied to Cymru Cenedlaethol/National Welsh with H45/32F bodywork. One of the ten, HR8211(MUH285X) is seen here shortly after delivery from ECW in March 1982 carrying fleet number HR1855. Later to be found in the Arriva Southend fleet as 5375, it then passed to the Arriva East Herts & Essex fleet. This Olympian had body 25117 carried on Leyland chassis ONLXB/1R ON252.

(Copyright Malcolm White/C. Keall)

The end of
Eastern Coach Works

Scenes recorded on 23rd January 1987.
Top Left-The empty Body Shop [Assembly].
Top Right-The empty Body Shop [Jigs].
(Both copyright Norman Fairhead)

Bottom Left-The last vehicle to leave ECW. Recorded on 30th January 1987.
(Copyright Norman Fairhead)

Some Eastern Coach Works Memorabilia (items not to scale)

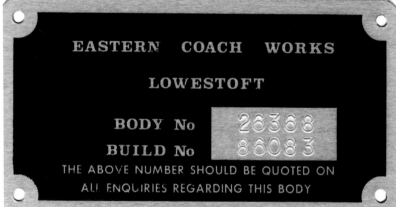

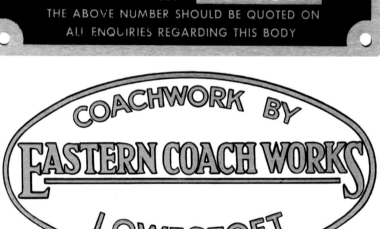

Top Left - External front body plate. **Centre Left** - Body Identification plate [For Midland Red South 962 (C962XVC)]. **Bottom Left** - Vehicle body internal transfer. **Top Right** - Builder's plate on Stagecoach 19952 (JAH552D). **Bottom Right** - Rare steel Bristol Tramway & Carriage Co. Ltd. label. Used when sending chassis parts and spares from Bristol to Lowestoft. Most of these heavy duty labels were discarded at Lowestoft.

```
LEYLAND BUS  BA716                                    DATE. 14/10/86
----------------------------------------------------------------------
                                  -

             BATCH 716 (1986) - RELEASE DATE & SANCTION 22 SEP (WK.39)
             ******************************************************

             34 - 9.65 METRE OLYMPIAN D/D BODIES ( 14'2" O/HT ) - LONDON R.T.
             ************************************************************

     -------------------------------------------------------------------------
     IBUILDI SERIALI   OPERATOR    I CONT.I BODY I    REMARKS     ICHASSISI
     I SEQ.I  NO. I                I NO. I NO. I                  I  NO. I
     I_____I_____I_____I_____I_____I_____I_____I
     I     I      I                I     I     I                  I       I
     I  1  I227/260ILONDON REG.TNSP.I12273MI 26567 I  CMO237 (87/120)ION.25921
     I  2  I228/260I       "        I   "  I 26568 I       "        ION.25931
     I  3  I229/260I       "        I   "  I 26569 I       "        ION.25941
     I  4  I230/260I       "        I   "  I 26570 I       "        ION.26001
     I  5  I231/260I       "        I   "  I 26571 I       "        ION.26011
     I  6  I232/260I       "        I   "  I 26572 I       "        ION.26021
     I  7  I233/260I       "        I   "  I 26573 I       "        ION.26031
     I  8  I234/260I       "        I   "  I 26574 I       "        ION.26041
     I  9  I235/260I       "        I   "  I 26575 I       "        ION.26051
     I 10  I236/260I       "        I   "  I 26576 I       "        ION.26061
     I 11  I237/260I       "        I   "  I 26577 I       "        ION.26071
     I 12  I238/260I       "        I   "  I 26578 I       "        ION.26081
     I 13  I239/260I       "        I   "  I 26579 I       "        ION.26091
     I 14  I240/260I       "        I   "  I 26580 I       "        ION.26151
     I 15  I241/260I       "        I   "  I 26581 I       "        ION.26161
     I 16  I242/260I       "        I   "  I 26582 I       "        ION.26171
     I 17  I243/260I       "        I   "  I 26583 I       "        ION.26181
     I 18  I244/260I       "        I   "  I 26584 I       "        ION.26191
     I 19  I245/260I       "        I   "  I 26585 I       "        ION.26201
     I 20  I246/260I       "        I   "  I 26586 I       "        ION.26211
     I 21  I247/260I       "        I   "  I 26587 I       "        ION.26221
     I 22  I248/260I       "        I   "  I 26588 I       "        ION.26231
     I 23  I249/260I       "        I   "  I 26589 I       "        ION.26241
     I 24  I250/260I       "        I   "  I 26590 I       "        ION.26301
     I 25  I251/260I       "        I   "  I 26591 I       "        ION.26311
     I 26  I252/260I       "        I   "  I 26592 I       "        ION.26321
     I 27  I253/260I       "        I   "  I 26593 I       "        ION.26331
     I 28  I254/260I       "        I   "  I 26594 I       "        ION.26341
     I 29  I255/260I       "        I   "  I 26595 I       "        ION.26401
     I 30  I256/260I       "        I   "  I 26596 I       "        ION.26411
     I 31  I257/260I       "        I   "  I 26597 I       "        ION.26421
     I 32  I258/260I       "        I   "  I 26598 I       "        ION.26431
     I 33  I259/260I       "        I   "  I 26599 I       "        ION.26441
     I 34  I260/260ITHAT'S ALL FOLKSI   "  I 26600 I*R.I.P.*  (120/120)ION.26451
     I_____I_____I_____I_____I_____I_____I_____I


                   PLANNED ASSY COMM. WEEK 45 - W/C 3 NOV
                   ========================================

                                        VBL NO. ZZK6314/-/179
                                        *************************

                   BATCH 716 (34 LRT)                THE END.
                   ******************                ********
```

Above Details of Batch 716, the last vehicles with ECW bodies
Top Left An ECW Timesheet
Bottom Right The "Hooter" Magazine for December 1953

VOL.2 No 43   SIXPENCE
DECEMBER, 1953
The CHRISTMAS HOOTER
OFFICIAL MAGAZINE OF THE EASTERN COACH WORKS SPORTS & SOCIAL CLUB, LOWESTOFT
LUCKY NUMBER 7

MESSAGE FROM THE PLANT DIRECTOR

ON BEHALF OF EVERYONE AT EASTERN COACH WORKS, MAY I WELCOME YOU
TO OUR FACTORY. WE DO HOPE YOU WILL ENJOY YOUR VISIT AROUND
OUR WORKS AND SEEING OUR LATEST BUSES AND COACHES, WHICH WE ARE
EXTREMELY PROUD TO EXHIBIT. YOU MAY BE INTERESTED TO KNOW
THAT OUR HISTORY IN THE INDUSTRY GOES BACK TO 1912 DURING WHICH
TIME WE HAVE PRODUCED OVER 26,000 VEHICLES.

THE BUS AND COACH MARKET HAS SEEN SOME DRAMATIC CHANGES IN
RECENT YEARS. THE CESSATION OF THE GOVERNMENT GRANT OF 50% ON
NEW BUS PURCHASES, COUPLED WITH THE PROPOSED DEREGULATION OF UK
BUS SERVICES HAS RESULTED IN A MARKET COLLAPSE FROM 2400
VEHICLES A YEAR IN 1980 TO A PROJECTED TOTAL OF UNDER 1000 FOR
1986.

OUR RESPONSE HAS BEEN POSITIVE IN OUR EFFORTS TO DEVELOP COACH
PRODUCTS AS WELL AS ATTACKING IMPORTANT OVERSEAS SALES. WE
HAVE HAD CONSIDERABLE SUCCESS IN OUR VENTURES IN GREECE, HONG
KONG AND AMERICA AND ARE HOPING FOR SUBSTANTIAL SALES IN
THAILAND. IN THE HOME MARKET WE ARE PLEASED TO BE SUPPLIERS
TO THE NATIONAL BUS COMPANY, LOTHIAN REGIONAL TRANSPORT AND IN
LOOKING FORWARD TO 1986, TO LONDON BUSES, WHEN 260 ECW OLYMPIANS
WILL BE SUPPLIED TO OUR CAPITAL CITY.

MY THANKS TODAY TO EVERYONE WHO HAS SUPPORTED THIS EVENT,
EMPLOYEES, SUPPLIERS AND LOCAL BUSINESSES. WE CAN ONLY JUDGE
OUR SUCCESS IN TERMS OF THE FUNDS WE RAISE FOR THE JAMES PAGET
HOSPITAL C.T.SCANNER APPEAL - SO PLEASE ENJOY YOURSELVES.

BEST WISHES.

P J MIDDLETON, PLANT DIRECTOR

EASTERN COACH WORKS SOCIAL CLUB WELCOMES YOU TO THEIR
FIRST OPEN DAY & FETE.

THE CLUB HAS BEEN IN EXISTANCE SINCE 1933, AND LIKE THE
COMPANY HAS HAD ITS UPS AND DOWNS IN THE PAST BUT THE
FUTURE LOOKS VERY PROMISING.

AS YOU ARE AWARE THE PROCEEDS OF TODAY WILL GO TO THE
C.T.SCANNER APPEAL. WE HOPE THAT AFTER YOUR TOUR OF THE
FACTORY YOU WILL MAKE YOUR WAY TO THE SPORTS GROUND, WHERE
THE UNDERMENTIONED STALLS AND ACTIVITIES HAVE BEEN LAID
OUT FOR YOUR ENJOYMENT AND ENTERTAINMENT. WE TRUST YOU
HAVE A GOOD AFTERNOON AND PLEASE GIVE GENEROUSLY.

LIST AT TIME OF GOING TO PRINT:-

36 VARIOUS STALLS, INCLUDING HOT DOG; BAR-B-Q BURGERS &
SAUSAGES; VEGETABLES; SOFT DRINKS; TEA; BEER MARQUEE; CAKES;
STRAWBERRIES; ICE CREAM; GAMES; HELIUM BALLOONS.
CHILDRENS GAMES AREA.
FIRE & AMBULANCE SERVICES

C BALDWIN
CHAIRMAN

LUCKY Nº   000365

Leyland
BUS

EASTERN COACH WORKS

OPEN DAY & FETE

ALL PROCEEDS TO
CT Scanner Appeal

SAT. JULY 20TH 1985
1.00PM — 5.00PM

Programme **25p**

★ PRIZE FOR WINNING PROGRAMME NUMBER -

14" B/W PORTABLE TELEVISION

This may be your
Lucky Number   Nº   36

Official Programme

Eastern Coach Works
Sports Club

ANNUAL SPORTS -

TO BE HELD AT

Norfolk Street, Lowestoft
On Saturday, 17th. July, 1948

Gates Open 1.30 p.m.

First Event 2.30 p.m.

Admission by Programme 1/6 (INCLUDING TAX)

The Lion Press, Lorne Park Road, South Lowestoft.   Phone 1133.

Menu:

"Feast and your halls are crowded,
Fast and the world goes by."
ELLA WHEELER WILCOX

SOUP:

CLEAR TURTLE
THICK OXTAIL

GRILLED SOLE MAITRE D'HOTEL

ROAST STUFFED TURKEY and HAM
CRANBERRY JELLY

CHATEAU and PUREE POTATOES
CAULIFLOWER AU BEURRE
BRUSSELS SPROUTS

FRUIT SUNDAE
COUPE NEAPOLITAN

BISCUITS and CHEESE

COFFEE

Toast List:

"He ceas'd; but left so pleasing on their ear
His voice, that list'ning still they seemed to hear."
ALEXANDER POPE

To propose   To respond

The Queen

THE CHAIRMAN

The Company, Ladies and Visitors

"I am fond of the company of ladies, I like their beauty,
I like their vivacity and I like their silence."
SAMUEL JOHNSON

THE CHAIRMAN   R. E. SUGDEN, Esq.

A. S. TATTERSALL, Esq.

                                        Esc

Toast Master—P. CHAPMAN, Esq.
Dancing to NEVILLE TURNER and His Organ
M.C.—V. A. CLEGG, Esq.

Committee :—
J. T. BALDWIN, *Chairman*
L. NICHOLS, *Secretary*   :   H. GREEN, *Treasurer*
P. CHAPMAN   :   A. HUKE   :   M. E. LLOYD

Top Left   Extract from the 1985 Open Day Programme
Top Centre   Open Day Programme
Top Right   1948 Sports Day Programme
Bottom Right   Menu for the Christmas Dinner held at
                     the Royal Hotel on 30th December 1954

PHOTOGRAPHIC INDEX
A selection of ECW bodied vehicles

Please Note - The operator shown in this index may not be the original, current or last owner.

At the same time as the redundancy programme was well under way, and just weeks before closure, the remaining work-force were being encouraged to "Get Things Right First Time-It pays the **Company**, it pays **You** and it pays the **Customer**". One day this comment appeared on the very last body !!!